Make Your Career Great Again!

All Secrets Revealed!

Make Your Career Great Again!

First Edition, 2017
Second Edition, 2018

Copyright © 2017, Richard Renstone

Published by Arthur Black Publishing

All Rights Reserved

Library of Congress Control Number: 2017934570

ISBN-10: 0-9979596-4-9

ISBN-13: 978-0-9979596-4-2

A copy made by anyone without permission from the copyright holder is an infringement of copyright and against the law. No part of this book may be reproduced, scanned or distributed in any printed or electronic form without consent of the copyright owner, or an agent authorized to do so.

Make Your Career Great Again!

Richard Renstone

Edited by

Dr. Rita Mukherjee and Renato Antolovich

Cover Design

Dr. Rita Mukherjee and Renato Antolovich

DEDICATIONS

To my loving wife, who has introduced me to real love, trust, hope, support, understanding, encouragement and so much more that I have never in my life experienced before.

My wife has made it possible for me to create all of the books that I have written and will write.

Thank you my love for loving me the way you do and for being my everything.

CONTENTS

DEDICATIONS	VII
CONTENTS	IX
INTRODUCTION	XI
THE EMPLOYEE	1
EMPLOYEE MINDSET	7
THE PROS AND CONS	21
THE SECRETS	107
BEST PRACTICES	143
IT'S A WRAP	311
ABOUT THE AUTHOR	313

x

INTRODUCTION

If you have this book in hand you may be a student in search of a summer job; or are close to graduation, excited to enter the professional work force; or an employee with a few or many years of experience. Are you searching for information regarding permanent employment and being an employee?

In that case, do you have a predicament at work or in your career, making you feel uncomfortable or awkward that you would like to change? Are you in anxiety and worrying a great deal about your career and future? Do you feel frustrated as if you're on a treadmill going nowhere? Are you feeling isolated? Maybe you're confused about the "system" at work that everyone understands accept you. Of course, these kinds of thoughts can make you feel as if you have lost your career mojo leaving you in self-doubt. Moreover, there is no one to talk to or any information to help you understand and change your situation. You just want to feel confident about yourself and your career.

Sadly many of you may feel like giving up hope, are ready to quit and find another job instead of trying to understand what happened or know what you could have done to change your career path. Don't worry you are not alone because there are millions of full-time permanent employees just like you that don't like their job, feel lost, puzzled, frustrated, upset, angry, anxious, have let their career spark go out, given up altogether, and just keep moving on working and changing jobs.

There are numerous work situations that involve drawbacks, risks, shocks and unforeseen circumstances that you want to be prepared for before they happen. Having factual information about what you may experience in your career helps you understand what you are getting yourself into, such as, potential obstacles, career stagnation, frustration and other circumstances that are out of your control. By now your information search has been empty because there are none on these subjects to give you the knowledge you need, until now.

Make Your Career Great Again! provides profound and practical insight to deal with various employee situations or circumstances that may arise throughout your career. How? It contains real stories based on decades of genuine employee experiences and circumstances. Each story is unique and evokes joy, excitement, laughter, heartbreak or anguish relating to employment situations that can happen to anyone. Make Your Career Great Again! provides you with the tools, experience and insight so you don't let yourself become scared, unable to cope but instead, have the power to break through any hurdles to continue on a career path you want! Now you have an opportunity to get your mojo back, expand your knowledge and understanding about employment, improve and enhance your career and livelihood by getting promotions and pay increases and more. Are you ready? Then do it!

MAKE YOUR CAREER
GREAT AGAIN!

PART I

Permanent Employment

and being a

Permanent Employee

Page Left Blank

THE EMPLOYEE

The employee is labelled by many people, employment agencies and companies, as a permanent employee, fulltime employee or just plain employee. However, the fulltime employee label doesn't work for me, since fulltime employment can be carried out whether or not the person is an employee or a consultant.

On the other hand, calling an employee, a permanent employee suggests that the worker is long-term, has an employer-employee relationship of some kind, meaning the worker displays a degree of commitment, stability, loyalty, security, and subordination. Also, the employee will perform duties according to the work schedule set out by the employer. Therefore, the employee will work any regular and irregular work hours the employer has set, and, the priority in which the employee performs their duties or responsibilities. Moreover, an employee must follow all corporate policies, standards, practices and procedures which includes employee pay scheme and pay period.

Employees receive pay according to the employer's pay schedule and policies. So, the permanent employee is dependent on the employer determining and controlling the amount of pay, the frequency of pay and the method in which the employee is paid. This means, the permanent employee is paid a wage for their service, usually a salary, which can be paid monthly, weekly, or bi-weekly usually on the 15th and 30th of the month, every second Friday or can even be a monthly payment. The rate of pay is usually calculated by using how many working days there are per year.

Most importantly, a permanent employee receives a NET paycheck, which is derived after many deductions are subtracted from the GROSS paycheck amount. The paycheck deductions all correspond to the employee's benefits package and government deduction requirements.

Initially, employee benefit package and government deductions include, but are not limited to, such items as:

- Medical
- Dental
- Accidental death
- Life insurance
- Long and short term disability
- Vision care
- Prescription drugs
- Psychologist sessions
- Massage therapy

- Physiotherapy
- Employee assistance services
- Paid holidays
- Paid floater days
- Paid sick days
- Federal taxes
- Provincial or state taxes
- Employment or unemployment insurance
- Pension plan coverage either company or government based or both, and
- Maternity leave

Medical costs and coverage vary because of government funding and other supplementary supports. Keep in mind that dental, medical and prescription drugs and other coverage will have variations based on age group, country, state, or province. For instance, in the United Kingdom medical coverage is free for all UK citizens. Dental coverage is free but only for certain individuals. To view additional dental coverage restrictions in the UK visit the following URL:

http://www.nhs.uk/chq/Pages/1786.aspx?CategoryID=74

Furthermore, in the United Kingdom, a permanent employee must seek and secure their own insurance for dental and prescription drug coverage since they are not free. However, there are exceptions. Prescription drugs are only free for any child up to 16 years of age and for seniors 60 years old and over.

Generally all benefit plan costs are deducted from an employee's paycheck with a few exceptions. For instance, if an employee had to purchase a benefits package from an insurance company as an individual, the cost would be substantially higher or even more than double. The reason is the benefit package an employee pays for is only a portion of the full cost, because the employer usually pays 50% or more of the total cost. However, when it comes to government related deductions, such as, pension plans and employment insurance, the employer pays at least double the costs even though this is obscure to the employee.

Some employee's benefits packages may also include, a company pension plan, or another type of retirement savings plan like, in Canada, a Registered Retirement Savings Plan (RRSP) or in the U.S. a 401K or in the United Kingdom, a private pension plan.

Any government based deductions are more geared towards state, provincial or federal taxes, government benefits or programs which include some items like, retirement pension, employment or unemployment insurance or national insurance and so on. The percentages for each deduction vary because they are calculated according to country of residence, marital status and the income amount. Employees must pay for all benefits package and government deductions because all of them are mandatory and to many employees the cost may seem high.

Keep in mind that many people are confused when looking at their paycheck and many just assume it is all tax and then wonder why taxes are so high. The reason is total deductions from an employee's GROSS paycheck will range from 28% to 50%. Note that these deductions include benefits package and government deductions so it's not only tax. For example, in the US, federal tax is at a rate of 11%, state tax is 4%, and social security is 6.2%. In Canada, federal tax is 10%, provincial is 7%, pension is 5% and employment insurance is 2%. Note that deduction percentages are all based on the employee's location, the amount of income, and marital status.

Therefore if the employee lives in Nevada or in South Carolina and so on, is married or not, will make a difference but also the higher the income the higher the deductions. Deductions are a part of what a permanent employee must pay for being an employee with benefits.

To find out more information about actual tax rates go to the following websites:

<u>For Canada:</u>

http://www.cra-arc.gc.ca/tx/ndvdls/fq/txrts-eng.html

<u>For the United States of America:</u>

http://www.irs.com/articles/2014-federal-tax-rates-personal-exemptions-and-standard-deductions

<u>For the United Kingdom:</u>

https://www.gov.uk/income-tax-rates/current-rates-and-allowances

So far we have reviewed some of the basics of being a permanent employee, by examining the work relationship, pay, and deductions, but that's not enough, since there are more gaps to uncover. Another main gap to explore is the employee mindset, which is actually what determines why people choose to be a permanent employee in the first place.

EMPLOYEE MINDSET

The employee mindset is a combination of many things that together, make a person become an employee. What I have found is employees generally stay long-term, for 20 to 30 years or more, which is a generational aspect that my parents retained, as well as, some of my generation.

This mindset was to get a job, work hard and stay with the same company until retirement, without the need for advancement and higher wages but just to be grateful for making a living and having a good job. These attitudes were based on fear and usually coming from an immigrant standpoint like my father and mother had. In the end, the permanent employee would finally retire only to find themselves in the grave a few years later.

So, is staying at the same job a disadvantage for people? The answer is, yes and no. I say this since it depends on the individual. Some people are happy to sit in the same job day after day and go with the flow which is generally union type jobs. On the other hand, others working in non-union type employment want to improve their lives and hop around in search of more opportunities with better environments, higher pay, and better benefits and so on.

However, workers who stay for their entire work life in non-union environments may at some point risk being phased out by technologies, or reach a point where they can't get a job elsewhere because they have allowed themselves to stagnate and lack the required skill sets. If employees continue to gain the required skills as they putter along in the same job, they generally are not at risk of being tossed a side but end up staying with the company.

Overall the main theme of employees is, they are individuals that require consistency, safety and security with very little drama and instability in their lives when it comes to their income, job security and especially retirement. This rational sets up employees to be loyal, making them cling to a long term employee type situation.

This employee mindset is generally based on feelings of insecurity, which is created by having current and future fears mainly about failure. Some of the negative biased thoughts or dialogue of the employee's mindset is based on negative or inaccurate thoughts something like:

- I don't want to lose my job, because I will have to start selling everything

- If I lose my job, I will lose my car, house, and everything else I have

- If I lose my job, I will lose my pension, maybe my spouse will leave me

- I can't cope with job expectations and stress, high output, efficiency and productivity

- I will be replaced when I get older then what do I do?

- I'll get fired because I do poorly at every job I do

- I'm stupid and can't get anything right…

- I was fired before and I don't want that to happen again

- I don't know where I can get another job like this one

- Got to pay my bills

- The company will take care of me

- I have company benefits, medical, dental, accidental death…that I need

- I can't lose my paid holidays, floater and sick days

- I belong to a union, I am protected, and guaranteed

- I am guaranteed 40 hours a week and a paycheck

- They can't replace me I've got a lot of experience here

- What will I do when I am retired, will I have money to retire?

- What happens if I die?

- Who will take care of me if I become sick or very ill and can't work?

- With all the economic downturns and instability at least I have a job

- The company is strong and will protect me from economic turmoil

- I have enough seniority now they can never get rid of me…

- I am committed to working for this company so they will do the same

- I don't want to have stress in my life; I just want to work until I retire

- I will get replaced by someone younger when I get older and lose my job

So, most of the employee's thoughts and beliefs are based on a negative future and are coming from within the individual. The employee achieves this by their thoughts predicting or projecting a negative future or outcome about their job, pay, income, old age, and retirement to name a few.

This thought process in psychological circles refers to anticipatory thoughts which in general terms signify the person anticipates a negative outcome in the future related to failure at their job, which could result in being fired, divorced, loss of their home, possessions, or no money at retirement or having no pension, and/or even getting some incapacitating illness, and so on.

These kinds of thoughts, consequently, create the worries, fear and anxiety the employees feel. The reality is these thoughts are generated within regardless of the person having no real concrete, or tangible evidence to have or support such thoughts. In essence, the employees are predictors of a negative future for themselves because they may have low, self-esteem, self-confidence and self-worth. These kinds of qualities are the basic building blocks for this kind of negatively biased mindset. Where does this employee bias and negativity start?

First of all, this employee mindset and choosing to become an employee usually starts at a very early age. Since, believe it or not, we all learn to play, "worker, employee or even business person" from our parent or parents. With that in mind, many permanent employee types are no different from their permanent employee parents. I say this because we all watch, listen and through osmosis, learn from our parents about defining what a job is, what working is, what a paycheck is, what hours to work, and how to make money. We also learn and see firsthand, all the associated feelings of frustration, anxiety, worry and anguish involved with employment, and money. We also record, the hardships and the attitudes our parents had about work and most importantly their fears.

As children we learn by listening to all the conversations and comments our parents make and discuss during breakfast, or at the supper table, or while watching television in the living room, or while speaking to their friends on the phone and so on. We also watch our parent or parent's work routines. For instance, we see them getting ready in the morning; having breakfast and coffee; packing their lunches and ours, setting off to go to work; to drop us off and pick us up from school or daycare; or if they bring work home with them, or have to stay late and on and on. This happens regardless, if our parents are teachers, lawyers, scientists, social workers, professors, programmers, engineers, plumbers, doctors, welders or whatever their profession is. Our parents also provide us with career and work information by speaking to us directly.

Practically all parents provide guidance, words of advice and wisdom to their child or children so they too will do the right thing in regard to employment and careers. Likewise, our parents may have a government job such as, a professor at a university or college, or work in a government office, or may have a union based job. From this, we are told or through osmosis to get a similar government based or union job just like our parents have.

After this kind of exposure and learning experience voila we, become a permanent employee because it's the right thing to do since, this is what kind of job our parents had. In other words, many of us have a similar job or career as our parents because through their influence and teachings, we inherit their mindset, opinions, insecurities, fears and anxiety about life and especially the workplace.

For instance, when I was growing up, my father was a plumber and of course always under stress and worrying about finances. A couple of my brothers wanted to be a plumber like my father, while another brother wanted to be a firefighter, and I wanted to be a medical doctor to help people.

Even with all of these childhood hopes and dreams we had, I remember my father specifically telling us to never be a plumber because it was a dirty and unhealthy job, even though at the time and even today it is a very lucrative trade to be in. Instead, we became engineers, managers, and consultants, but first we all became permanent employees just like our parents.

Dealing with the Fears

After working as a permanent employee at many companies I observed and found some of the factors involved that helped many employees alleviate their fears, worries and anxiety and it started with becoming a permanent employee.

First of all employees are, "permanent". If we look at the dictionary meaning of "permanent" it states, "a long lasting or intended to last or remain unchanged indefinitely". Interestingly enough, just the word "permanent" itself, projects commitment which is fulfilled and supported by the employee-employer relationship that exists.

This relationship can be compared to any intimate relationships we are familiar with such as, friendships, marriages, and so on which also establish the sense of safety, trust, and security. A permanent employee position also paves the path to feeling that nothing will change and therefore having no need to worry which in fact keeps all fears and anxiety at reasonable levels.

Can you recall the first time you were showing up to a new job, like how nervous, scared and anxious you were? Having sweaty palms, and maybe even some stomach or digestive problems, because everything was new and you didn't know anyone. After being at the job for a month or so, all of it gradually disappears. The reason, you start to relax and become familiar with co-workers, your job, and have developed routines. More importantly you surpassed that nail biting three month probationary period.

Employees also use repetition and familiarity to ease their workplace anxiety, tension and fears. Employees accomplish this by staying at a job for many years to attain a senior level of experience where they learn all aspects of it. They perform the same tasks and decisions day after day and during that period form long-term relationships with co-workers. All people, including myself like to feel comfortable, with very little worry or doubt, in fact we all seem to thrive for familiarity, at the workplace and at home. Most of us also need to establish routines in all areas of life, both personal and professional, since it provides a means of familiarity, consistency and stability.

For instance, a routine at work may be, as soon as you get there, you see Rita in the elevator and you both have a short chat about the game last night. Then you get off the elevator proceed down the hall toward your desk or office, then, you look into Ted's office to see him at his desk, and say good morning. You arrive at your office, take your jacket off, turn on the computer, get up and go to the coffee room with "your" personal coffee cup to get a coffee…

As employees, there are no sudden surprises or confusion, since we have already surpassed those. We all know the coffee machine location and who Bill is, what Julie does and that both of them are on the third floor and why Judy talks like that to everyone or that Hank is always grumpy... All of these things are familiar and routine, making employees feel comfortable in their surroundings and workplace settings.

This familiarity and feeling comfortable reminds me of a short story about how I made a new hire feel comfortable. I remember working for a field service company and I was a senior employee and was a smoker at the time. All the smokers would smoke at this table that was set out in the back shop area away from all the offices.

At this workplace, many of the employees would play soccer during the lunch period as long as there were enough people to form two teams. I can recall on a Tuesday, anyone that was available went out to play a game of soccer. However during this lunchtime game it was different. One of the players, Richard, was running fiercely after the ball to find out when he looked up, he slammed his face into a fence post. This poor fellow broke his nose, had two black eyes and drove his front bottom teeth through the skin between his lower lip and chin which required over 25 stitches. Richard was an easy going person, a happy-go-lucky sort of attitude but this situation was very unfortunate.

Later that afternoon, when he returned from the hospital, you could see his whole face was swollen, black, blue and red, absolutely awful and looked very painful. He had some difficulty in speaking since his bottom lip and face was so swollen but you could still understand him. Nonetheless, he was in good spirits knowing that it would all eventually heal.

The following day, I arrived at work and had a cup of coffee in hand and was standing at the smoking table having a cigarette. All of the sudden a horn sounded telling me that someone was at the front door wanting to get in. I put my coffee down and immediately walked over to see it was a new hire, Phil. The operations manager told us about Phil the day before.

So, I opened the door and shook his hand and said, "Good morning Phil, I'm Rick, welcome aboard, can I get you a cup of coffee or something?" He looked shy and nervous and said, "Well…ah…sure that would be great, um… is there any place… where I can put my lunch and then have a smoke?" We went into the coffee room and he placed his lunch in the fridge, grabbed a cup of coffee and we went into the back shop to the smoking table.

We were standing at the smoking table drinking coffee and talking about what it is like to work at this company, then discussed the training he would receive and all the documentation that he could review that day, just to get him feeling comfortable and bring him up to speed. I could empathize with being at work the first day on the job, all nervous and unsure not knowing anyone or what lies ahead or if you'll fit in and so on… We continued with smoking and talking and he was feeling quite relaxed.

So here I was making this new hire, Phil feel comfortable and relaxed then I heard the back door slam. I didn't know who it was because many people used the back door to get to their office. The person who arrived turned out to be Richard, and he was walking toward us.

As Richard approached us, we could see how gruesome and beat up he looked, with his face swollen, black and blue with stitches. At that moment, I looked right at Richard pointing and shaking my finger at him, I said, "And the next time you son-of-a-bitch it's gonna be a lot worse!" Of course, Richard being the happy go lucky guy he was, joined into the act and started shaking as if he was scared and then briskly ran through the doorway.

I looked at Phil, he had no pigment in his face, white with fright, scared out of his mind, he was shaking, avoiding eye contact, and confused. I am sure he was wondering how this psychopath could beat this person to a pulp and still be employed.

Anyway, I looked at Phil again and said, "Relaaax" and started laughing. I immediately started telling him the truth behind what happened to Richard and his soccer accident. Phil let out a big sigh of relief, and calmed down and started to laugh. He said, "Wow, I was really scared of you after seeing what Richard looked like." I replied, "Hey no worries shit like that doesn't happen here I was just trying to get a laugh".

Other personal routines we have to make us feel comfortable may be after work like; going to pick up your kids from daycare or your parents' house, and while driving home you talk to your kids about their day. Then you arrive home, your kids run into the house ahead of you; you get in the door, make a cup of tea or coffee or have a beer, sit down turn on the television, or read the newspaper.

You relax, for about a half hour or so, then you get up and start making supper, and your spouse shows up and so on. Of course, we all have important routines that we need in order to feel comfortable. There are other things that make us feel comfortable especially like being a permanent employee with a benefits package.

The employee benefits package calms many fears and reassures that they are covered and taken care of, in case of any unexpected medical, dental, accidental death, or serious illness that leaves an employee unable to work, or to have huge unaffordable medical bills. The employee benefits packages support the employee which in turn makes them feel safe and secure.

Another form of calming fears is employees are also locked into a regular paycheck with paid holidays, and sick days. The employees always know they will be paid every two weeks without any worries about losing the regular pay which again reinforces the feelings of commitment and security. In fact when it comes to a paycheck the employee can almost set their watch to the time they receive their pay.

Another reassurance the permanent employee has is that they have a connection that they are a part of a group, a family and department. Additionally, the permanent employee is also accepted, acknowledged for their voice, opinion, experience and knowledge. This again, ensures the employee that they are valued and worthy of the position they hold which helps their self-esteem and self-worth.

Lastly employees have a pension plan for their retirement. Retirement for many is a thought process of being taken care of in their later years with no financial or medical upheavals. An employee's pension alleviates the fear they have about their future retirement.

All of these points we have discussed so far add up to taking care of the employee's needs so they feel safe, secure, have the ability to forecast into a stable future, to know that there will always be another pay check and in the end a pension. These were some of the norms I had in my mind at one point that made me feel stable, secure, reduced the worries about life, finances and my future.

After discussing the general mindset that drives employees, we still have to fill a huge gap with regards to the advantages and disadvantages are when being a permanent employee. I found that these are what make employees, employees.

THE PROS AND CONS

After all the experiences I have had as an employee, I found there were many advantages to it but also many disadvantages. In this section, I will discuss contrasts that exist when being an employee. Keep in mind that we all have different upbringings, focus, values and morality which all play a role in forming our outlook on life and work. Some of you may feel that being an employee has no disadvantages, or that there may be a few to add to the ones I discuss.

Your views and experiences may be different from what I point out because being an employee may work for you entirely. I believe that people in general have to do whatever works for them. However, with any role, there are advantages and disadvantages, and most importantly if the disadvantages outweigh the advantages, we tend to look for another option, like an alternative role or job or look for something completely different.

So, first let's explore some of the advantages we all have as permanent employees.

Richard Renstone

Page Left Blank

EMPLOYEE ADVANTAGES

In this section I discuss some of the employee advantages that I have found and experienced while being a permanent employee. All of these advantages may vary depending on the country, state or province you live in, as well as, working for a particular company or corporation. Even though geographic location somewhat influences these advantages I have listed, they are still applicable and are very similar in nature because the human factor plays a significant role.

REGULAR PAY

One advantage I found when working as an employee was receiving a regular paycheck like clockwork. This was money, a source of income I would receive usually every two weeks or bi-weekly, like on the 15th and the 30th of every month or every 2nd Friday. Sometimes, depending on the company, some employees can even be paid weekly but that is quite rare and I didn't personally ever experience it.

The consistency in paychecks to me, was fantastic, a regular paycheck to keep me from worrying about money, bills and other related stuff. This is one of the elements that provided consistency and foresight for me as an employee and fulfilled one of my needs that I could always count on.

DENTAL COVERAGE

Dental coverage is a part of an employee's benefits package and is helpful, except that there are some limitations and restrictions on coverage. Nonetheless, I found that the cost for crowns and other dental appliances are covered up to 50%. This is still an exceptional deal since employees are getting a discount on basic dental work and each six month cleaning and check-up that provides the employee with incentive to ensure they have excellent dental health. At one point, I found the larger the company you work for the better dental coverage you would have, however now all dental coverage is very similar.

EXTENDED MEDICAL COVERAGE

Extended medical coverage is also a part of the employee benefits package and includes, ninety percent coverage on prescription drugs and a certain coverage amount for other items such as, psychology sessions, massage and physio therapy, and so on. The medical coverage one receives does differ based on geographic location, the insurance company and their actual employer.

For instance, in the US, the company you work for will usually provide you with a medical plan but keep in mind you may have to purchase additional coverage.

If you live in the United Kingdom, almost all medical is covered by the government and is free, but items like prescription drugs and dental work are not covered. Therefore an employee in the UK will have to find separate prescription drug and dental coverage.

In Canada, employees rely on the medical coverage supplied by the employer, but also must pay for provincial medical coverage that is mandatory. Payments for this coverage vary in each province. For example, in Alberta there is no charge, while Ontario residents must pay via direct paycheck deductions or by using other financial channels.

Overall this coverage is still positive, regardless if paying for it or not, because as we all know, we need it.

LIFE, ACCIDENTAL DEATH AND DISMEMBERMENT

This is another employee benefit, which is intended to protect them and their family in the event of accidental death or dismemberment. The coverage depends on location of course but also is based on salary, which is used to calculate what payout amount would be granted in case of sudden or accidental death. Usually the awarded amount is two times the employee's salary if the employee dies or has total paralysis. This payout is a bonus either way you look at it since, this could help your loved ones to carry on, as well as, cover funeral costs, personal debt and other associated costs without worry.

PENSION PLAN

A pension plan in my opinion is the most important part of being an employee. Pension plan benefits are also one of the main reasons why people are employed with a company for life. The pension plan in fact equates to, the employee being taken care of in their later years. This I feel is one of the top advantages of being an employee if you get the right company and pension plan.

So, which pension is the right one? Pension plans have a couple of different schemes. The first one is when the employer matches the employee's contribution up to a certain yearly limit. Employee contributions are regularly deducted from the employee's paycheck. The other pension scheme involves the company having its own pension plan which still requires employee contributions that are deducted from the employee's paycheck. However, this scheme pays the employee a specific amount at retirement. These two pension schemes are the most popular types and are called defined contribution pension and defined benefit pension respectively.

In my opinion, a defined benefit program is the best one to choose because this plan has a set income amount the employee will receive after 20, 30, or 40 years of service.

In this situation the employer has made a commitment to take care of its employee through setting aside a sum of money, a pension fund that is used for employee pensions. The employee has no worries or doesn't have to make any decisions just stay with the company for the minimum amount of time required in order to receive their pension. The amount of pension employees receive is based on factors like tenure at the company, number of years contributed to the pension plan and what their average salary was in the last 5 years of employment. However, I have seen this pension scheme fade away quickly from the pension world.

The defined contribution pension is becoming more common because it's up to the employee to make decisions based on what shares, mutual funds and other investment instruments they will use to invest for their own future, and pension fund. In this schema, employees contribute and then the company contributes matching a percentage of the employee's contribution to a maximum yearly amount.

Any of these pension schemes are a decent plan regardless if they are defined benefit or contribution. In addition, any of these pension plans are especially beneficial for those individuals who have problems saving money for their future retirement.

STOCK OPTIONS

I have worked for a few companies that offered stock options. Options are generally a good deal anywhere you work, at least most of the time. Stock options are mainly used to,

- Offer employees additional financial compensation

- Retain and attract employees

- Provide a profitable incentive for those employees who purchase Call Stock Options

- To help the company's stock price rise

- Make employees feel like owners or partners in the company they work for and

- Provide confidence to the employee about the company and its future

Employee stock options are comparable to stock exchange traded call options but issued by the employer. In simple terms a call option means that the person who buys them believes the stock price will rise. In the past, options were offered to executive management. Now more and more companies offer stock options to all of their employee's as a part of the employee benefits package and as a form of supplementary compensation.

The employee can buy options by deductions off their paycheck, or can purchase them outright. When the employee purchases stock options, they have the right to purchase a set of company stocks after a certain timeframe or vesting period, and at a set price or strike price which is all determined by the employer. The set price of the option is called the strike price and is ordinarily set at the current market price or a higher price than the current market price of the stocks (shares). The vesting period for the options is usually set at a future date. In order for the employee to exercise the option or convert the options into shares two conditions must be met. First the vesting period date must be expired and second, the current stock price must be higher than the strike price.

For example, an employee decides to purchase 100 stock options which allow the employee the right but not obligation to purchase 100 company shares. The company has set the strike price to $10 per share, with a vesting period of one year. The employee will pay for the options by paycheck deductions. This means the employee allows the company to deduct the amount of the cost of 100 shares at $10 each for a total of $1000 from their paycheck. These payments from their paycheck are in increments of $200 bi-weekly. After five weeks the employee owns the options. This gives the employee the option to buy 100 shares of the company stock at a strike price of $10 per share. The vesting period set on the option to buy the shares at $10 per share is one year from the date the employee received the options.

At this point, the current stock price is $8 per share so the employee cannot exercise their options because the two conditions have not been met. During the one year vesting period the employee has been monitoring the stock price and has seen it rise to $25 per share and now the one year vesting period is expired. At this time, the employee exercises their options meaning the employee converts the options into shares and is free to sell or do what they wish with the shares. In this case, the employee decides to sell 100 shares at $25 a share for a profit of $15 per share or $1,500 profit minus any commissions. Keep in mind that there are many variations on company stock options and any profit or capital gains on the shares are taxed according to government regulations and laws.

Regardless of commissions and taxes stock options in my opinion are an excellent bonus and are a good balance for added employee compensation. When dealing with stock options I have never lost money myself nor have seen anyone else lose money.

However make an important note when dealing with stock options:

(1) Keep in mind that with any market trading there is always risk of losses

(2) If by chance the employee lost their job or got fired during the vesting period, they lose the stock options since the contract is usually void.

PAID HOLIDAYS

Holidays…finally…let's pack up and go! Paid holidays are the norm for any permanent employee.

Generally the employee is restricted to a minimum of two weeks of paid holidays in the beginning of their employment; however some companies start their new employees at three weeks. Make note that a week of holidays is really five working days off not seven.

As an employee continues to work year after year, they continue to accumulate and increase holiday length at certain yearly milestones. For example, an employee after five years of service increments their holidays from two weeks to three weeks and after 10 years of service from three weeks to four weeks. After 20 years of service the employee is given another week to bring it to a total of five weeks holidays. The positive spin on holidays is the employee is paid full wages for each day of their holidays, so there is no interruption of income.

I can recall at one point employees could stack their holidays year after year. Some coworkers would never take holidays for periods up to 20 years, thus accumulating a large amount of holidays. Unfortunately today employers have caught on to this and have stopped or restricted this practice, generally making employees take their holidays each year. Keep in mind that each company is different and has its own policies that govern employee holidays.

PAID SICK DAYS

In addition to paid holidays, employees have another advantage which is paid sick days. Usually companies provide an employee with 10 to 12 sick days per year but of course this will differ from company to company. Sick days are working days used anytime an employee is ill and must stay home. When the employee is at home sick they are paid full wages for each sick day thus having no pay disruptions or loss of pay.

Companies at one point would allow employees to stack their sick days if they were not used. However, I have found that companies are phasing out this policy, since numerous employees would stack sick days for decades because they never get sick or sick enough to stay home. They would then use these stacked sick days and stacked holidays to take early retirement at full wage for a few months before their pension commences.

Now most companies have changed their policy so employees will lose their sick days if they are not used during the year. However, some companies allow employees to carry over some of their sick days to the following year but that's as far as they go, otherwise if they are not used they are lost.

I recall a little story about when I was working for a government based entity and all the employees had a very similar mindset about sick days. I remember taking a couple of sick days because I was ill with a bad cold. When I returned to work, a few coworkers approached me and asked, "Where were you these past couple days?" I said, "Well I was sick I had a bad cold so I took couple of sick days" they replied "What! What are you doing?

Why waste a paid day off when you can use those days for mental health days to get away from here and enjoy yourself instead."

PAID FLOATER DAYS

Paid floater days are an advantage and a part of the employee benefits package. Each year the employee has a set number of paid floater or personal days which is usually 10 to 12 days per year but the amount will vary since they are set by company policy. So floater days allow the employee to avoid having a loss of income or pay disruptions. These floater days can be used at the employee's discretion but generally people use them for personal incidentals.

Incidentals most times require the employee to attend or to be somewhere during regular working hours, such as, car repair, a child's graduation, weddings, cable installation, furnace repair or maintenance, day surgery and so on.

These were also stackable just like the sick days and holidays, but many companies again are steering away from this practice too. Consequently, employees must use the floaters days before year-end otherwise they lose them.

PAID TRAINING

Training for each employee is paid for by the company or the employee pays out of pocket then to be reimbursed. During training the employee is paid their regular wage and do not lose any pay. In addition, the company will pay for all training expenses and associated costs which cover items such as, training materials, travel, accommodations, flights, meals, car rentals and other items.

The company will provide and pay for training courses that are internal, external or third party. Any of the courses can be in classroom, or online such as, eLearning, pre-recorded or live webinar. Additionally, the company will purchase, training material such as books, videos, DVDs, and audio recordings. Training material supported by the company pertains to topics specific to the company and its employees. Some training topics may be, ISO 9001, ITIL, project management, risk management, change management, company policies, cost engineering, various certifications, quality assurance, self-improvement, ethics and software courses and so on.

Training is a bonus for any employee because many training courses are usually very expensive and provide the employee with the opportunity of adding new skill sets or updating current ones that can immediately be used on the job thus making employees a valuable asset.

JOB SECURITY

The definition of "job security" is set by each individual since it's whatever it means to the individual. I say this because most people have their own interpretation and definition of what it means. Generally, employees feel that security means their employer provides lifelong employment so they will not lose their job, and have a steady paycheck. This also includes having regular salary increases usually 2% to 3% that are based on merit or cost of living or both. Security also involves a pension plan and other benefits that cover medical, dental, paid holidays, sick days, floater days , etc. and all of this is a wonderful recipe for having a sense of security.

Having security keeps employees comfortable with their work life, pay and feel life is easier. The majority of permanent employees are usually searching for secure jobs within large companies, or government entities that are unionized. The reason is once employed by these large companies, especially union based jobs; they can effortlessly acquire any kind of credit. Some of the credit vehicles include such items as, mortgages, lines of credit, credit cards or any other credit instruments they wish to have.

Additionally, this advantage allows employees to enjoy security, since it helps them from worrying about their future, losing their job or income and know they will always be employed until they retire, which could be as long as 20 to 40 years or a lifetime.

UNION

I have worked a couple of union based jobs and I recall one was for a government agency. I found that working there was okay, the people and environment was acceptable too. What I found was this type of job was mainly for individuals that only want to work for a company, have a position and were not driven or looking for career advancement. By this I am referring to those individuals who need security, a steady income, benefits, and the support and strength of a union. Moreover, they don't mind just doing the same job day in day out, because it supports the employee feeling secure about their job and livelihood.

When I was at this job, working in maintenance, I found it was merely impossible to get fired, since I saw people, stealing packages and boxes, package contents, credit cards, and some even making death threats. What would happen to these individuals? The union would intervene; the employee would be given a short suspension with or without pay and then be reinstated shortly after.

This practice only reinforces the employee's sense of security since it is like being untouchable, and don't lose their job, regardless of the circumstances. This of course I have never agreed with, since there must be limits and consequences for employee's actions. Consequently, as unionized employees we were able to do almost anything without problems or the threat of losing our jobs.

For instance, I was on night shift based on having the lowest union seniority level. Regardless, I tried making the best of it and having fun like I do at any other job I have had. I recall working the night shift in the plant and we were ahead of schedule with our tasks. A co-worker, Lester and I, started to make up an entertainment plan. As a joke, we wanted to leave something for the day shift that started at 7 am. While we were in the back area of the maintenance shop, I lay down on the floor with my left arm bent at 90 degrees from the elbow facing up and my right arm bent, at 90 degrees facing downward. My legs were positioned with my left leg straight and the right leg bent at 90 degrees with my heel almost touching my butt. As soon as I was in position, Lester proceeded to outline my body on the floor with masking tape just as they do on the murder-mystery crime shows you see on TV.

While Lester was outlining, another coworker from a different department was walking by and stopped. They asked if the person on the floor was okay and I immediately lifted my head, laughed and stated that it was all good. Then the coworker came over to see what we were up to; as they got closer you could hear laughter get louder and louder. We completed our masking tape masterpiece and were proud of our accomplishment. Finally our shift came to an end and the day shift started. Many on the day shift were amused by this gift we had left on the floor. On top of it all we received many compliments for our creative work.

Another thing to add is that it was against the law for any employee to be drug tested because it was against their rights. Is that security or what? You can be an employee with numerous substance abuse problems, be under the influence and keep getting paid without any consequences. Of course, there are always exceptions to the rule, such as being employed as an aviation or health care professional and so on which brings up another example.

CAREER ADVANCEMENT

First career advancement depends on the company and the structure it has in place. So in this section I will only focus on discussing non-union type companies because unions have a seniority structure. In an ideal world, employees generally can move up the career ladder, because of their performance, quality of work, productivity, professionalism, interpersonal skills, education, training, and years of experience.

Career advancement can happen rapidly in a public or private sector, within non-unionized companies, because there are usually new opportunities being created due to rapid rate of expansion and growth, employee movement and turnover, and having a progressive structure in place. Public and private sector companies in most cases are open to providing solid pathways for employees so they can advance their career, attain higher status and gain higher pay.

For instance, while I was working for a public traded field service company, I was able to catapult my career from a trainee to a junior level within seven months, surpassing the average period of 12 to 18 months. Then continued to advance to an international technical advisor position within 2 ½ years. This advancement was phenomenal and proof of a career pathway, since international employment was usually offered to senior employees with a minimum of 7 to 10 years of experience.

The other side of career advancement is all up to the individual. Some people want to advance into new or different positions while others are happy just doing the same job with slow movement if any. Advancement in a career is based on how determined, ambitious, and driven the person is, as well as, their interpersonal skills, expectations, needs and most importantly their values.

Career advancement is a huge benefit for all employees as long as it is exactly what they are looking for, as it advances people into different career positions and salary increases, elevating a person's livelihood and lifestyle.

NO LIABILITY

When employees are working at the office, in the shop, or out in a field location, there is always some kind of risk or liability. However, an employee generally has no worries about additional expenses for liability or attaining coverage because the employee is fully covered for any liabilities by their employer. General third party liability insurance covers such items as,

- Injuries to customers, employees, vendors or visitors that occur at the company workplace

- Injuries that have occurred outside the company's workplace that resulted because of an employee's actions from negligence

- Third party property damage caused by the company's employee

Some employers are insured through an insurance company while very large companies can be self-insured.

LONG TERM FORECASTING

Long term forecasting is usually made by corporations and companies in respect to their financial outlook and business strategies. However, as far as permanent employees are concerned, they have steady and verified income, especially when they are working for a large company, government entity and/or unionized employer. A permanent employee has an advantage to forecast long-term income since the income is the same for each bi-weekly or monthly pay period for years into the future.

With this in mind, it is quite normal for employees to plan for long term goals and purchases, since their income and job is considered by banking institutions to be very stable. However, banks require that an employee has worked at the same company for at least 6 months to 2 years. As long as they qualify, banks are generally wide open to provide credit proportional to the employee's income level.

With long term forecasting in mind, employees in unionized or government based jobs tend to take on long-term debt to make large purchases such as homes, fifth wheels, campers, jet skis, motorcycles, and other toys they feel are necessary. These union and/or government employees fit right into the "buy now pay later" scheme of things that is offered everywhere.

CORE AND KEY PERSONNEL

Core personnel are the individuals that make up a large group within a company that are considered as the foundation of the company's employee base. These individuals all play minor and major roles within the company and are permanent employees who continue to work with no thoughts of ever moving or leaving the company.

There is another elite group referred to as key personnel and only certain employees are considered as key personnel. This elite group makes up a vital body, making important and critical departmental, group or company decisions that affect the department, division or company as a whole, both administratively and financially. This means that this group is responsible for the company's future actions going forward.

People that are usually selected for this key group are senior individuals who are keeners, with high productivity, genuinely committed, with excellent job performance and interpersonal skills. The employees are highly motivated, knowledgeable, experienced and are team players. Usually the key personnel group includes people who are CEOs, VPs, directors, senior management, and senior personnel. Now how is that for status?

I recall working for an inspection company, when I was chosen to be the lead person trained on the highest technological and most current instrument the company had designed. I was trained in the field by the senior electronics engineer and the senior scientist. We would perform services with the instrument and would encounter instrument design problems. As a group we would come up with solutions and ideas to iron out the design flaws and problems.

After this training and testing period, a support crew and I conducted services with this instrument around the world. I spent a few years breaking the international market with this instrument and produced all the training and support documentation. After that I became a part of the elite key personnel group. This group consisted of the CEO, manager of operations, head of research and development, lead design engineers, senior scientists as well as, myself and a few other senior level field staff. We were making decisions that controlled the company's future, such as policy, standards, procedures, strategic brainstorming, training requirements, human resources issues and other decisions.

When I reached this level of recognition, it made me feel important and special, that I was actually chosen as one of the top employees to make company decisions on policy that would affect the company's future. In fact, it was motivating and overwhelming. It made me want to work for the company even more and to do a better job than I was already doing.

Page Left Blank

EMPLOYEE DISADVANTAGES

After reviewing and discussing all those advantages, I am sure you are ready to explore the disadvantages. These disadvantages I have found are many and hopefully will not be a shocker. In essence what works for each person is up to the individual. I say this because some of you may feel there may be none at all, or disagree with some I have listed or if there is any, they may be so puny that it's a waste of time. In this section, I will discuss some of the things I found were disadvantages when I was a permanent employee.

YOUR HOURS

As an employee you are obligated to work at minimum within a range of 37 to 44 hours per week. The company requires employees to work this range of hours because most employees pay is calculated on a yearly basis, including all working days and statutory holidays. This information is then broken down into monthly, bi-weekly and hourly pay. Therefore, missing a couple hours of work is unacceptable as far as the accounting department is concerned, because each employee is paid according to the calculated yearly formula.

So, if these mandatory set hours are broken up by the employee taking a few hours off, it is generally frowned upon since it alters the calculated salary resulting in the employee owing the company hours. In this situation, the employee is tracked by administrative staff to ensure the employee makes up the few hours that were lost. This tracking and chasing done by an administrative support person in my experience generally is comparable to a parent chasing a child about the hours they owe.

The employee must work extra hours to make up for the hours they owe; however, these makeup hours are not regular hours but considered overtime as they are outside of normal working hours. Overtime hours and are usually paid at time and a half or double time, but not in this case. In fact, the employee takes regular time off only to give the company back overtime hours. How does that work? It doesn't benefit the employee because it's almost like a penalty for taking time off.

Another lost hour scenario to add to this is the employee may be forced to take a floater day in lieu to cover the lost time. Is this type of scenario fair? In my humble opinion, trading a whole day for a few hours isn't fair at all.

To me it seems like a sure disadvantage and frustrating, being chased around by the admin and forced to work overtime hours in lieu of or to take a full floater day off when only a couple hours are at stake.

LOW PAY

As an employee, companies pay lower wages based on the remuneration which includes combining a wage, plus the full benefits package which represents the employee's entire compensation package. Each company has their own cost calculation for how much the benefit packages cost per year. However, according to the U.S. Department of Labor the employees benefit package alone can account for up to 30 percent of the total remuneration.

For instance, if the employee is single and has a paid salary of $50,000 per year, the benefits package could be worth an additional $15,000 making the full remuneration, $65,000 per year. Are the benefits you are paying for really worth $15,000 per year or more? Probably not, since many of us don't have the need to use the full benefits package. For instance, some employees never get sick; don't take holidays, or use prescription drugs, may not require glasses, and have excellent dental heath already, don't buy stock options, or contribute to a 401K or RRSP and so on. Consequently these employees are paying for the benefits package anyway. As an employee you are forced to take a lower wage because of the total remuneration package regardless if you want it or not, or if you use it or not, since it's mandatory.

UNION STUFF

Of course, a union environment has some benefits such as, protecting its members from unfair treatment related to pension, wages, work hours, health, safety, training, wrongful dismissals and other work related issues.

With union protection also comes, workplace drawbacks, for those employees who want more from the employer. Those who would like to have more pay, better options, opportunities, and career advancement. All of these are not possible in a union environment. The reason is any sort of opportunity for anyone is given to those who have worked there the longest and have the most seniority, if they're qualified or not.

I recall when it came to holidays; I would have to wait to choose my holiday days. Finally when it was my turn, there really wasn't much left since I was only able to choose from October and November. This wasn't a good time for camping or any other good weather stuff.

Moreover, I couldn't work the day shift with everyone else or the afternoon shift but had to go to midnights or grave yard shift, 11:00 pm to 7:00 am. I couldn't move to another shift, unless someone with higher seniority chose to work midnights for some reason, quit point blank or died before I could actually work day shift. Also, even if any of these situations did happen there was always someone else with more seniority regardless if they worked in the same city or not. In other words, I was stuck on midnight shift for years or possibly decades.

There is also another catch to being unionized, which entails going on strike. This is when all union members stop work and form a line outside the company to protest about something that the union feels is unfair or needs. Usually these union disputes are in regard to wages, benefits, pension plans and so on. However, during a strike, union members lose their full wage and some receive a supplementary payment while others don't. So losing wages because someone or some people decide to go on strike is a disadvantage. Also, many of the members don't want to go on strike and have no awareness of the strike but show-up against their wishes anyway. Keep in mind that strikes can last for years or the company can even close down.

For instance, an article by the Wall Street Journal clearly explains the effects union strikes can have where no one wins and everyone loses. The article, called " Hostess Closes Plants as Workers Strike" states that "Three days of labor strikes have prompted Hostess Brands Inc. to close three plants and mull a possible liquidation of the beleaguered baking company." This is only one example in regard to the negative impact a strike can have. If you would like to read this article, go to the following URL:

www.wsj.com/articles/SB10001424127887324439804578114862262799942

Another point is I found that many people choose union employment so they can hide from real jobs, do minimal work, get paid, and cannot get fired. Additionally, these are employees who are very inefficient, have low productivity, are carefree that are protected and paid regardless of their output, attitude, looks, drug and alcohol addictions, psychological problems or other things. These people are what non-union based company employees would call, "dead wood." These dead wood types in non-union environments would get fired instead of being retained.

So, if you are an employee working with these dead wood types and have high efficiency, do an excellent job, are professional, highly productive, keen, an idea generated, organizer, and team player, it doesn't matter. Since you are paid like the next person regardless of performance. Besides that "dead wood" will become your supervisor eventually. To put this another way, you get paid the same as Mary, Bill or Joe that do the minimal amount of work, only bitch and complain, create problems and use the protection of the union to the fullest extent they possibly can and keep screwing everything up all the time and don't care.

The only thing dividing you from them is your pride, performance, quality of work, self-worth and self-image. So, how can someone be happy knowing that this actually exists while getting paid the same as others who are entirely different with negative attitudes that just create trouble? It's called union! Also, if the company decided to downsize its union employee size you will get laid off while they stay employed.

TRAINING

Most employers provide training for their employees with internal or external courses, that are online, eLearning or in classroom. The employer will cover costs only for training that pertains to enhancing the employee's knowledge; skill sets or for certifications as long as it is relative to the employee's job. Some employers pay for training their employees are pursuing that is outside of the standard courses being offered by the company. Before the company agrees to pay for such training courses or certifications, the employer will set up contract obligations with their employees. One of the obligations set by the company is to have the employee guarantee they will work for the employer for a set term after they have successfully completed the training.

For instance, an employee wants to take a course on supply chain management or a six sigma black-belt for a certification and have it paid by the company. The company sets up a contract obligation whereby the employee must work for the company for at least 2 years after successfully obtaining the certificate.

This contract obligation is set up by the employer to ensure their employee stays and applies the new acquired skills in their current position and prevent them from running to another company for more pay with their new acquired skills and certification.

Another contractual obligation the employer may require is a minimum average passing grade of 80 percent or more. If the minimum grade requirement is met or exceeded, the employer will pay for the courses. However, if they fail to achieve this then the employee must pay back the company for the course cost in full or via paycheck deductions. On the other hand, if the employee paid the course costs upfront then the employee will have to personally absorb the costs.

These contract terms are put in place to provide drive and incentive for the employee. However, when the company pays for the employee's courses, the costs will be added to the employee's income tax statement, as a taxable benefit found on tax forms W-2 in the USA, T4 in Canada and a P60 in the UK.

This means at year end, the course cost is added to the employee's salary, having the employee pay any required taxes. On the other hand, if the employee personally paid for the education, they may include this as a personal income tax deduction. The training provider or institute must provide a tax receipt for income tax purposes. Also be aware that the IRS, CRA and HMRC place restrictions on what kind of personal income tax claims are allowable for education, tuition and textbooks and so on. So it's up to you to do your own due diligence. One more point about training is it's always up to the employee's manager or supervisor to decide which courses the employee can take. Generally, employees are only allowed to take courses that are directly in alignment with their current job and this is also dependent on their work schedule and availability. Therefore, if there is a conflict with course time and work schedule, the employee's request for training is rejected.

Another aspect about training deals with an employee wishing to change jobs by adding new skills unrelated to their current position or are courses that are career changing in nature. Most times these types of courses do not align with the company criteria and are declined. The reason is the supervisor or manager may feel that they are, irrelevant, do not add value to the employee's current position or the employee would use the training to transfer to another department.

In other words, in these circumstances the employees are stuck in the same job, even though the courses do benefit the company and employee. As a result employees will have to pay for the course on their own. Additionally, if the employee is trying to make a career change even within the company it is still quite difficult in most circumstances because, most major career changing courses are held at universities or colleges that require daily in class attendance during work hours like 8 am to 4 pm. Many courses are offered on line but overall it becomes very difficult to complete courses due to time restrictions, finances or personal obligations thus becoming another dead end for the employee.

ADDITIONAL BENEFITS

Additional benefits or sometimes called "fringe" benefits an employee may receive could be training, company car, golf membership, cell phone, tablet or car allowance and so on. Fringe benefits at first seem like an awesome perk, but that is only until you find out that they are deemed as a taxable benefit by the HMRC, IRS and CRA.

The employer must add the cost of these benefits to the employee's yearly income tax statement and these benefits are all taxed accordingly. Generally, the amount that is added to your income is money that has not been taxed, and may result in pushing the employee into a higher tax bracket. Meanwhile, the employee usually has no awareness of this benefit being added to their total income.

So what commonly happens is that after the employees taxes are complete they get a wonderful surprise from their accountant stating, "You owe $8000 on your taxes, sorry but that's how the numbers crunched out for last year." This means that the employee must pay the income tax bill to the IRS, CRA or HMRC. Then of course, the employee's response to this is, "WTF is that? 8000 bucks I thought I was getting a refund? How did this happen and where am I going to get 8 grand?"

The amounts added to the employee's income tax statement will vary and correspond to what kind of benefit it is. I have found that vehicles or company cars/trucks that are used fulltime by the employee for both personal and business is one of the largest and quite expensive. Especially if the company pays for all expenses for the vehicle such as insurance, fuel, maintenance and repairs. Also some golf memberships can be very expensive as well as training courses as I mentioned in the prior section. As a rule of thumb the more cost an extra benefit has the more the employee will pay the tax man.

In Canada for company vehicles there are two components used to calculate the tax benefit amount, the standby charge and the operating cost benefit. The standby charge is derived by 2% of the original vehicles market value, plus sales tax and another calculation for length of time the vehicle is available to the employee which is represented by months.

For example, an employee has a company truck with a total market value of $60,000 including tax, which is used for field service and personal use. The vehicle is available 12 months a year because the employee drives it for both business and personal and parks it at home every night. So the calculation for standby charge would be:

Standby Charge is equal to:

2% X ORIGINAL VALUE OF VEHICLE + TAXES X MONTHS AVAILABLE

Or,

.02 x $60,000 x 12 = $14,400

After arriving at a standby charge $14,400, an operating expense benefit is calculated.

The operating cost benefit has two different calculation methods. One method accounts for flat kilometer charges of $0.26 cents per kilometer and the other is choosing half the standby charge. For example, to calculate the operating cost amount we use the flat kilometer charge and 23,000 personal kilometers. The kilometer use is based on less than 50% personal use. The calculation for the total operating cost is:

Total Operating cost = 23,000 x $0.26 = $5980.00

For the total amount of taxable benefit the employee is taxed is:

Total Benefit is equal to:

Standby Charge + Operating Expense Benefit

=$14,400 + $5980

=$20,380

In this case the employer would add $20,380 to the employee's income on top of the regular salary of $70,000. The salary and taxable benefit brings the total income amount to $90,300. However, the employee has only paid tax on $70,000 with regular deductions and the amount of tax required for a $90,300 income is what the employee must pay to the CRA. In this case the difference the employee will pay is about $10,000 to the CRA...surprise!

To find out more information go to the following URLs:

In Canada,

http://www.cra-arc.gc.ca/automotor-benefits/

For some fun use the online CRA Automobile Benefits Calculator at the following URL:

http://www.cra-arc.gc.ca/autobenefits-calculator/

In the US, a company car or vehicle is also taxed accordingly. The method used is based on personal usage of the car as compared to business usage. If the employee uses the car 45% of the time for personal use then this is multiplied by the market value of the vehicle of $40,000. So the total fringe benefit for this company vehicle would calculate as follows:

Personal Usage Percentage x Car Cost

=.45 x $40,000

=$18,000

The employee in this circumstance would have a fringe benefit of $18,000 added to their income tax statement and taxed accordingly.

For more information about fringe benefits go to the following URLs:

https://www.irs.gov/publications/p15b/ar02.html

http://smallbusiness.chron.com/calculate-imputed-income-company-car-20112.html

However, in the UK the calculations are more complex because of breaking down specifics about the company vehicle, which includes, the manufacturer, model, engine size, fuel type, trim, year and plate, tax year and tax rate.

For more information regarding a company car benefit in the UK go to the following URLS:

https://www.gov.uk/calculate-tax-on-company-cars

https://www.gov.uk/tax-company-benefits/tax-on-company-cars

Or have some fun by using this company car calculator.

http://www.parkers.co.uk/company-cars/tax-calculator/

The whole idea about additional benefits is that the employee is taxed because of the personal component or usage.

Again, it is very important to do your own due diligence by asking an accountant or calling your local tax preparer, CRA, IRS or HMRC offices to find out what the consequences are of taking on these benefits. They may seem wonderful at the time, until you realize you are paying for them at tax time. I feel that this surprise of paying a huge tax bill is a total disadvantage.

THE COMMUTE

Employees commute on a daily basis from home to work and return. Some of the fortunate people live in close proximity to their workplace while others are faced with lengthy commutes via car, rail, bus or taxi. When it comes to commuting, there are a few factors to strongly consider like, the time it takes to commute, lost time and cost.

Commute and Lost Time

When it comes to actual commute time, an employee may work in the city center; work in a suburb or even a small rural town just outside a main city. Employees driving to work are faced with extended commute times because of situations such as, rush hour traffic, accidents, traffic jams, parking congestion, road conditions, weather conditions and construction. Therefore, employees must tolerate a return commute that may take one to three hours or more.

For instance, if the employee works from 8:00 am to 4:00 pm, then we can assume personal time is from 4:00 pm to midnight to do any personal stuff. In other words, an employee only has eight hours of personal time on workdays, if that.

Hence, if the commute is based on a range of 1 to 3 hours per day, and 22 working days per month, then each month the employee loses a range of 22 to 66 personal time hours per month. If we consider 8 hours of personal time to be defined as a personal day, it suggests when calculating this, that the employee can lose, 3 to 9 personal days per month.

If we extrapolate a little further and calculate for an entire year, then the accumulated lost personal time on the low end of the scale is, 22 hours x 12 equaling 264 hours. On the high end of the scale of lost personal time, if we calculate 66 hours x 12 equaling 792 hours. Therefore, lost personal time ranges from 264 to 792 hours per year or 33 to 99 personal days per year or from 1 to 3 months per year. Some food for thought to mention that is even more shocking is... what if we add all this personal lost time over the employee's entire work life of 40 years.

This Is Time Gone...Never To Be Recovered Ever!

Commute Costs

When an employee uses their car for commuting, costs rise for fuel, maintenance and repairs, then add in additional wear and tear, high mileage as well as having no car to use because of repair downtime. These result in degrading the reliability of the car, increasing the age and condition of the car, while drastically reducing its value. For example, when the car value is significantly reduced it could mean that the employee is paying a car loan for a $20,000 car while it's only worth $9,000. As a permanent employee all car expenses cannot be claimed as an income tax expense making the employee personally eat the costs.

However, if the employee decides not to drive and reduces commute costs by using alternative methods instead such as, light rail transit, bus, or taxi, the employee is still paying out of pocket expenses which again cannot be claimed as an expense on their income tax. Moreover, by using different types of transportation the employee may be extending the commute time thus losing more personal time or may even cut travel time. Cutting travel time can happen but overall it may make no difference due to train, transit or utility equipment failures, accidents, equipment maintenance and other delays.

Also, when the employee is paying for travel to and from the work location it is paid for by the employee using their net income. This is like paying another tax on top of the taxes they have already paid because they are using their NET pay. The cost to commute to the job location is all very costly any way you slice it. Commute costs can add up to a hundreds of dollars per year or more.

For instance, if an employee drives a round trip of 30 miles to work each day then if we extrapolate by using 22 working days per month. The calculation is 22 x 30 equaling 660 miles per month or 7920 miles per year. Note that this mileage is only for work and doesn't include mileage for shopping, travel, appointments and other personal usage.

Consequently, the longer the commute time, the more costly it is and increases the amount of lost personal time. Gee, I wonder why we don't have time during the week to do a lot of things like fix the fence, go for dinner, go to a movie, grocery shopping, take a course, learn a new language, and so on. A final note is this doesn't factor in extra work time employees have to put in, due to job demands and deadlines, reducing personal time even more. This actually reminds me of a story about commuting when I was a Technical Manager.

Coffee to Go

As a manager I would commute but also would quite frequently drive round trip twice a day. This would mean that I would be driving 40 miles per day and when being called in for problems would increase the mileage to 80 miles per day. I estimate that total mileage was around 300 to 350 miles per week or roughly 1200 to 1600 miles per month. These were miles I could not claim on my income tax, nor the fuel cost or the wear and tear on my car. At the time I didn't care much since I was driving a four door Reliant K car that had a small 4 cylinder motor with over 250,000 miles on it and still had excellent fuel economy.

Driving 20 miles to work would give me enough time to grab a large black coffee at a drive-thru coffee shop before embarking to work. Every morning I would drink a large coffee and throw the empty paper cup into the back seat area. This continued for over 6 months until I was shockingly pulled over by the police.

I couldn't believe that I was pulled over since I wasn't driving erratically or speeding or breaking any laws. Puzzled, I rolled down my window and waited for the police officer. The officer stood at my driver's side window and I could see him look into the back seat area.

Then he asked, "Can I see your driver's license and insurance?" I immediately handed it over. He went back to his car to check my registration and that everything was in order.

He started to approach the car and I could see him glancing at the back seat area. He handed back all of my paper work and while looking into the back seat area he asked, "Do you travel a lot?" I was sort of confused with the question but said, "Yes I do, travel every day because I live in main city and work in the small city just down the highway." Then I saw him look into the back seat again. So I asked, "Why do you ask about travel?"

After I asked I knew…it was the coffee cups that filled the entire back seat area that were almost pouring into the front seat. Then with laughter I said, "Oh shit I get it…all those coffee cups in the back seat right?" He smiled and said, "Yes I just thought I would ask." Then I asked, "Is there a problem officer because I wasn't speeding or anything and feel sort of confused why I would be pulled over." He said, "Your plate sticker has expired" and I replied with concern, "Oh my God, expired aren't they supposed to send a notification?" He said, "Yes unless you recently moved." I replied, "Oh shit, yes I did recently move about 5 months ago." He said okay that makes sense." I curiously asked, "How expired is my plate a couple weeks? Then he replied," Try six months." I responded, "Oh, oh now what?" The officer said, "I'll tell you what, you update your plate registration, go to the local police station with this slip I am giving you and show proof of registration and you'll be good to go, no fine but get this done as soon as you can." I took a deep breath smiled and said, "Thanks for the break officer I'll do that immediately." Note that an unregistered vehicle could be towed on the spot while you find a way to get back home.

PARKING

Parking usually is not an issue for employees that don't drive to work or when parking is paid for or provided by the employer. The employer pays for or provides parking only if the employer is located in a suburb, in a small rural town outside the main city or a location outside the city core like in an industrial area and so on.

However, when the employer is located in the downtown area, companies do not pay for employee parking. Actually throughout my experiences I have never had an employer cover parking costs in the downtown area which can be very expensive ranging from $200 to $1000 per month.

This all depends on the city and the location in the city. Parking costs are not considered as an employment expense, so the employee cannot claim this deduction on their personal income tax even though the employee again uses their NET pay to pay for another type of indirect tax called parking.

SALARY CLUSTER

Another disadvantage I have experienced stems from being a salaried employee. Companies generally calculate salaries by using working days over a one year period, then to arrive at a monthly salary and an hourly rate. This is calculated over an annual period because each year will have variations in how many working days there are due to statutory and public holiday placement. For example, in the US, in 2015 there were 240 working days while in 2016 there is 251 working days. With that in mind, some salaried employees who work overtime time hours are paid time and half or double time while other salaried employees are not paid for any overtime or extra hours.

An employee being paid overtime hours is up to the company and its policies, even though the employer has to abide by local, state, provincial or federal labor laws. Be aware that when an employee is hired, the employee usually signs an employment agreement which may override some labor laws. I am not going to explore government labor laws since it is beyond the scope of this book.

Nonetheless, there are companies that do not pay their employees any overtime instead they are paid their regular salary, with no extra pay or time off in lieu. Salaried employees are expected to work any hours required by their employer, in order to get the job done, regardless of the day, the time or amount of hours they put in.

Companies justify this type of salaried practice mainly by a tradeoff of paid floater days an employee receives which the employer feels will cover any accrued overtime. This may seem fair but what happens when the company you work for doesn't have any floater days or the extra hours worked exceeds the amount of floaters days? As a salaried employee, the employee has no choice because this is part of their employment agreement they signed. Therefore, it is in the best interest of the employee to do their own due diligence to ensure they know exactly what they are signing.

Another point is, when an employee works overtime hours they are compensated by being paid, time and half or double time. The reason is the employee works outside of regular work hours, using their personal time. However, when a salaried employee works overtime they are actually trading overtime hours for regular hour since floater days are regular pay. Is this situation fair? Sure it is, for the employer, not for the employee.

I was fortunate enough to experience this salaried employee kind of stuff first hand. I recall at my first salaried employment, that I didn't understand what I was getting into. The salary was, paid every month, but it was broken-down to a mid-month paycheck which was considered an advance, and it was usually a smaller amount than the end of the month paycheck. Nonetheless, I thought this was excellent especially when

I saw the salary amount because it was the most I was ever paid as an employee.

Life was great, huge salary, however I had no idea what was coming next. I didn't care much about anything because I assumed that the amount of hours that I would put in, would work out with the amount of salary I was getting paid, besides the salary was ginormous!

At this supervisor job, I first started working 5 days a week in the shop from 8 am to 5 pm. After some training I was shifted out to the field. At that point, I realized that the hours I worked were changing and started to ramp up. In fact, it turned out that this wonderful salary that I was receiving when calculated out on an hourly basis turned out to be significantly reduced. This is how it played out.

As a simple example, usually employees will work anywhere from 37 to 44 hours per week, which is considered a normal range. So if the employee is paid $20 per hour it equates to roughly $41,600 per annum, $3,467 per month or $800 per 40 hour work week based on 5 days per week, 8 hours a day. Keep in mind that each company has their own method of calculating salary for their employees. When a salaried employee not paid for overtime starts to work more than the base hours per week this suddenly reduces their hourly calculated rate because their salary amount remains the same.

In my personal example, I was working 14 to 16 hours a day in the field, 7 days a week. This on the low end works out to 14 x 7 or 98 hours per week and on the high end 16 x 7 or 112 hours per week. If I use the $800 per week salary amount, it's not a $20 per hour job anymore. The reason is I was not working 40 hours per week but instead a range of 98 to 112 hours. When using the same salary amount and the increased work hours to calculate the hourly rate it's not $20 per hour, but substantially reduced to 800 divided by 98 or 112 to arrive at an hourly rate range of $7.14 to $8.16 per hour. This to my surprise was less than half of the pay that I agreed to. I can't emphasize this enough, do your own due diligence and find out what you are actually signing.

After experiencing a salaried employee position like this one, I made it mandatory, to either work for an hourly rate or if being paid a salary that it is still calculated at an hourly rate and to be paid overtime rates of time and a half. Every salaried position I was offered that didn't pay overtime, I without hesitation outright refused.

TRAVEL TIME

Travel time to and from various work locations may not seem to be an issue especially if there is no travel involved with the employee's current job. However, when employees travel as a part of their job, companies usually do not pay for any extra time the employee travels, outside their regular work hours. Travel time for employees is not covered since employers feel that this is a part of their job, covered by their benefits and floater days. Does this trade-off of floater days sound familiar?

For instance, I recall travelling to a northern city to attend a full day meeting. A colleague and I, after working from 7:00 am to 3:00 pm, drove to the location arriving at the hotel, after 7:00 pm. This was unpaid time and amounted to 4 hours of overtime. The next day we attended the meeting which ran from 8:00 am to 4:00 pm then left to return home. While driving back, there was an accident that shut down the highway and delayed our return until the accident was cleared. This return trip normally would take about 4 hours but with the accident it took us an additional 2 hours so we didn't get back until 10:00 pm. This was another 6 hours of overtime to add to the trip, making it a total of 10 hours of overtime that the company would not pay for.

If we do some simple calculations for this loss of 10 hours of overtime and multiply it by 1.5 it equals 15 hours of regular time. This is almost equivalent to two full floater days. Hey, I thought floater days were supposed to be an advantage for employees!

Another example, was while working for an international service company, we were flying to locations all over the world. The field support crew of 4 to 5 employees would travel to their locations but never get paid for the time spent travelling. One way travel time could range from 8 hours to a couple of days.

If you do the math and calculate this for a whole year this adds up to weeks of unpaid travel time. This situation was in my opinion completely unreasonable and I discussed it with the manager of operations. I wrote a complete report of existing field related problems and their solutions. When presenting this report to the manager of operations he clearly understood the problems and the tension it was creating with all field staff.

In turn, the manager distributed this report to the CEO and other senior management to successfully change the current situation. The changes were, to pay for travel based on a flat daily rate, as well as, introducing a pay multiplier for each country of origin. The multiplier was based on the countries living conditions, length of stay, instability, and level of risk. It was a common practice to be in countries for at least 2 to 3 months at any one time.

At least in this circumstance I was able to change the pay structure for many of the field operational aspects of the company, but most times companies don't change their policies and unfortunately, have the "take it or leave it" attitude. So, travel time results in a substantial amount of hours that are unpaid which can be a very significant financial loss for the employee especially if the travel frequency is high. This by far is a clear disadvantage for the employee. Have you ever lived out of a suitcase for more than a week or two? It gets old very quickly.

WEALTH EFFECT

Wealth effect is about people, who become wealthy, and it doesn't matter where in the world they live, nor does it have any bearing on how many kids or children they have, what kind of childhood they experienced, education level, age, gender, the position they hold or the pay they receive.

First of all, wealthy doesn't mean someone who has a big house or drives a Mercedes or Porsche. Since, those may be people who make enough money and spend it all making payments, so they don't really own anything. This is not real wealth but only appears that way.

On the other hand, wealthy people do not make purchases like buying huge houses, extravagant cars, and depreciating assets unless they are extremely wealthy. The wealthy, buy moderate sized houses don't focus on purchases, like the latest gadgets, and need stuff; their focus is on living their life with family and close friends. They also are frequently looking for financial opportunities. However, middle class employees have a different focus in regard to money, buying and needing stuff.

Generally, employees focus on comfort and safety as I discussed earlier which equates to having it as easy as possible, by having a secure job, and working for someone else. When you are an employee, it means that, you are not going to become wealthy.

The reason is that the salary or hourly wage the employee receives when working in a union or other jobs are within the lower middle to middle class income range. This means that many employees are neither rich nor poor, but instead are comfortable. Also, employees are generally set up in the main stream of minimal savings because three quarters of their wealth is tied up in the value of their homes, and there is more to the picture.

Middle range income earners also take on long-term debt, to fall right into the "buy now and pay later' scheme that actually fits into most employee's way of thinking. According to a Bloomberg View article which states, "As of 2013, the average debt of middle-class families -- those that fall within the middle three-fifths of the population by earnings -- amounted to an estimated 122 percent of annual income, according to the Federal Reserve."

If you are interested in more information about consumer debt, check out the Federal Reserve report website at:

http://www.federalreserve.gov/econresdata/scf/scfindex.htm

Commonly, middle range income earners are shopaholics, taking on debt related to stuff they don't really need since they like to show off, and are generally in competition with the Johnson's or their other neighbors, the Kirfuknicks.

These middle income earners tend to live way above their means by buying huge houses, and cottages. Moreover, they are in an endless chase to have and possess the latest toys and technology. During their pursuit for goods they spend money on items such as, depreciating assets like cars, fifth wheels, campers, cell phones, tablets, televisions, surround sound systems, gaming systems, and other toys. The employees also can't have basic cable but want a full cable package and the highest speed internet access available. Shortly after, the depreciating assets are sold for a fraction of the cost to buy the newer model or thrown in the garbage or are passed on to some charity. Keep in mind that giving to any reputable charity or cause is always a good thing.

Of course these same people ask and wonder why they aren't wealthy. It's clearly because they have a different focus than the real wealthy do. Hey, don't get me wrong here since I am not being judgmental. People must do what works for them. Besides, there are always exceptions for example, some standup, change their mindset and focus on wealth building but most do not. This cycle of paying bills and adding more toys, then paying more bills is detrimental to employees and they never really acquire any real wealth but only debt and toys that lose value.

This is clearly a disadvantage in my opinion because the wealth effect I am discussing is based on employee mindset and the heart of it is safety. With safety there is no risk therefore no chance of taking any risk that may have a life changing outcome. Why do you think millionaires and billionaires are wealthy? They take risks.

BIG GUARANTEES

Employees generally believe in a few guarantees, a regular paycheck, their job and pension. After working as an employee for public, private and government unionized companies, I have formed some different views and thoughts about job and pension guarantees.

Employees feel that being in a permanent job working for a private, public, non-union or union company is an advantage and secure. However, they don't realize that they can be released or fired just as easily as any consultant or contractor or in fact can be released before a temporary worker, contractor or consultant.

The difference between how secure the union and non-union permanent employee's job is, boils down to two simple things. First the employee working for a non-union company can be fired by the employer for any reason or even "no reason" at all but cannot fire the employee for any reason that is discriminatory or retaliatory in nature.

The second is in regard to a union employee getting fired, which is a little more difficult but can be done successfully as long as the employer has handled the situation correctly. By this, the employer is compliant with the collective agreement, and any governing and arbitral legislation. Additionally, by following the correct routes employers also have the right to downsize their current unionized workforce size at any time.

In truth, union or non-union, no employee is exempt from losing their job nor guaranteed a job. The end result usually is the employee receives a compensation package and must pay tax on it. However if they don't receive a package or it's a wrongful dismissal the employee will usually seek legal counsel and establish a law suit against the company for wrongful dismissal. This results in the company paying a lump sum which goes to the lawyer, who gets paid very well and to the employee, and then it's over. So, even after the litigation, and arbitration the employee has still lost their job regardless.

I found out about guarantees the hard way while working for a large non-union company. This is a personal example of mine when I was a Technical Manager for a large field service company. I use this example because it clearly shows the, ruthless, calculated, carefree, and sociopathic behaviors of senior management and how employees may be treated. This is one example of my experiences about guarantees and this is when I changed my beliefs and mindset.

It all started when I was approached by an oilfield service company that was having loads of field operations problems. After being approached several times by a friend who worked there as a sales rep, I decided to accept the technical manager position. I agreed to take on this efficiency improvement adventure which I believed would advance my career but also mostly to help a friend. My friend's sales world was crumbling due to operational failures and nightmares, resulting from the company's market share slowly collapsing and the company losing $2 million a month in revenue.

At the time this company didn't pose as competition to other companies since its operational efficiency was around 40 percent if that. So in other words, every time they attempted to provide field service they would have a gong show and get run off the work location by the client. In turn the client would immediately replace this company with a competing company that was in the vicinity that had the ability to efficiently perform the same services. This kind of situation made it clear that, efficiency problems required some exploration.

After working for three months at this company and performing analysis, I was of course shocked with the findings and it all made sense. No wonder this company was failing at almost every service they performed. Upon completing my failure analysis, the operations manager announced that I would be the new Technical Manager and taking over the repair, maintenance and lab group. After this I had several general meetings with all staff to announce the future changes I would be making to improve the operational efficiencies. I also would conduct small meetings with field engineers and the technical staff to explain the benefits of my strategies and how the processes I created would be applied and used.

In addition to the changes, a bonus system was also introduced to all technical lab staff which was based on operational efficiency levels, for example: at 60% operational efficiency a bonus of 60% of the employee's salary would be paid, at 70%, 70 % is paid and so on. This in fact was a huge carrot and driver the technical staff had in place, because bonus was extra money on top of salary, and overtime.

With the research about the company's operations in hand, I went full speed ahead with a plan. I started to write a number of memos to a point where people started calling me "memo man". These were the first step to putting procedures and some controls in place for operational maintenance and repairs. I created and implemented forms to be filled out by shop and field staff to make measurements in the system. This was to generate some metrics so I could have a look at where we are now, develop a baseline and then to monitor our progress.

A couple of weeks later, I had a meeting with the operations manager to inform him that I required two additional staff. The first person I hired was a past co-worker to join our team since he knew the path to bring us to excellence. The next day I hired my ex-coworker, Barry Jones, got him a good base salary and he joined the team within two weeks. For the second person, I had HR run an ad then within two weeks I began interviewing potential candidates. I found almost everyone seemed to lack the enthusiasm, drive, and knowledge I was looking for. Then I interviewed, Brenda Bates, who was a tech graduate was driven, bright, very willing to learn and to join the team. I hired her, as I felt she was a keener and in the end my intuition was correct.

My staff and I were making substantial changes that transformed all the old operational processes into new efficient ones. As a rule of thumb, with any kind of change people usually start to feel fear and it creates anxiety. To try and ease the anxiety, I would put on training presentations to explain what we are doing, why and how we are changing things to get to our end goal and how it benefits everyone. Of course, these were changes that many current employees didn't like regardless of how you explained it. I found it really didn't make any difference since I was dealing with many old school employees that were there for over 20 years doing the same thing. Their mindset was, "Why fix something when it isn't broke?" as they perceived of the company's performance.

Even after providing multiple information seminars and Q&A sessions, it was still an uphill battle all the way with very few people on the positive side of change. Nonetheless, my staff and I continued to push the company into the right direction and to a different level of operation and service. As time progressed, I tackled many design flaws in some of the instruments which were a large part of the equipment failures and finally started to see operational efficiencies slowly rise. The lab and field staff started to acknowledge that operations were changing to the positive, as equipment failure was being reduced, in turn raising people's confidence. They started to have hope and confidence in their equipment and the support staff. This was the most satisfying for me. They were amazed and thrilled at the turning point. After a long, grueling and tedious fight this was finally coming to fruition, we were all on our way, since the trend had distinctly changed.

The operational efficiencies continued on their journey upward and people started to recognize the impact that the team and I had made. People didn't fight change anymore but welcomed it. The lab staff was pleased when they started to get bonuses which kicked in at 60% efficiency while the field engineers were making more money because the equipment and operational efficiencies were reliable. The field engineer's bonus was coming in at full force, as it should have, years ago.

Everything started to fall in to place just as I had expected, and the biggest payoff was to have people experience first-hand, the real tangible proof of the effects and results of changes that were made. Failures were becoming a thing of the past and a new future was taking hold. This paved a clear path of confidence that swept throughout the field, lab staff, and owners of the company. The time, effort and plan put in place to stabilize operations, correct engineering design problems, and lab procedures turned out to be very effective. So effective that it gave this company a long overdue face-lift.

Efficiencies continued to climb and there was no forecast only real numbers. It continued to increase month by month, and after 9 months we were sitting at over ninety percent operational efficiency. I was proud of the team for helping me achieve what I was hired to do. This was a huge, stressful and painful undertaking that took, many hours of overtime, frustration, fighting and arguing with people, as well as, introducing innovating ideas and business analysis acumen and problem solving. Yes, I stood proud because what I set out to do actually surpassed the level that I envisioned. After a long and tedious road I was on top of the world. I bought a new car, the first new car I had ever owned since I felt great with the achievements, felt confident in my job outlook and secure in my position. I received a letter of praise from the CEO and from the Manager of Research and Development. So here I was on top of the world just after 12 months of being there…but at the same time there were other things happening in my personal life.

On the personal side of things, my mother at 62, found out she had bowel cancer and it was far too advanced and was given two weeks to live.

Nonetheless, she continued with chemo therapy which kept her alive for 2 more years but according to her, it only gave her one day a month of feeling good. This went on until her passing. She passed, and my father was devastated by the loss of his soul mate of over 40 years. He setup her funeral and had her body placed in a mausoleum. I had taken a couple days off work to attend her funeral. Completely devastated, I went to her funeral and was overwhelmed with pain, loss, grief, and anguish, wondering why this would happen to someone like her at the age of 64. She, never smoked, drank just worked hard and loved her children. After attending her funeral that Friday, I returned to work the following Monday morning.

Professionally, I was on top of the world but devastated on the personal front with the loss of my mother. That morning I focused on my job since, that was the only positive thing I had in my life. After working about an hour or so, the operations manager asked me to come to his office to talk. At 9:30 am, I walked up the stairs and sat down in his office, looking at him, thinking that he was going to express his condolences about the loss of my mother but it wasn't the case.

He looked at me with a blank expression and said, "After some review, I find that you don't fit into the business model or the company anymore so I am letting you go." I was confused. Then after a few seconds I responded in anger, "What! You are getting rid of me after all of the stuff that I have done here, that I accomplished for this company, the stress and frustrations and anxiety! All the crap I have put up with fighting and arguing with people" I continued, "You can't do this to me this is a wrongful dismissal!" The manager said, "Ah...Please grab your things if you have anything here and the safety manager will escort you out, thanks."

Can you believe it, fired, no severance package or anything just fired on the spot, with no notice. What happened to all the things I did for this company? After all the time, effort, frustrations, disappointments and anguish I went through to achieve and deliver this level of operational efficiency then to only be thrown away like a worthless piece of garbage.

On top of it all, this bomb was dropped two days after my mother's funeral. Immediately questions started to go through my head like, what kind of a company was I working for that would do this? What kind of cold hearted people are these? How could I work for people like this? Why did I do this for such people who just used and exploited me? All this hard work for their benefit, what did I gain? I thought that if they did the same thing to someone else, that person might return to the workplace but with a gun to take care of business. Me, I would never do something like that.

After all of that effort, I finally achieved a 95% efficiency level which in turn, created an incredibly recognizable facelift to the company. In other words, when a company has current efficiencies levels of 90 percent and they rise to 95% there is not much of a noticeable difference. However, when you are at an operational efficiency of 40% to jump to 95% within 12 months, this is a huge contrast and extremely noticeable. Past clients were shocked by an enormous turnaround in the company's operational efficiencies and this created a massive increase in market share, competitive edge, creating tens of millions of dollars in new and future contracts. Clients were instilled with confidence, because a whole new image of the company was created.

I, on the other hand, felt devastated by my mother's death and about being fired. Now I was feeling, angry, heartbroken, disappointed, and betrayed. This made me feel worthless, unwanted and unworthy of other jobs. I was also worried about losing my first brand new car, from defaulting on car loan payments now that I didn't have a job.

After a while, I eventually stood up and pursued the company for a wrongful dismissal but the lawyer I hired took advantage of my anger. In the end the lawyer received $7,000 and I got $8,000 for the wrongful dismissal. So after all of that, what was it all worth? It was worth nothing. This only proves that any person regardless of their position, union or non-union, can be like one of those disposable staff as you see on Star-trek or other TV shows. In truth, companies can fire you for whatever reason they feel, if any and the ramifications are nothing.

The truth is, for the company, to pay an employee off with $20,000 or even $50,000 means nothing to them, because they move on while the employee's life is shattered. Sure I received many letters of praise from the owners of the company, CEO, and Manager of Research and Development, but it didn't mean anything in the end, because it was all for their benefit and the company's not mine. This company's facelift produced millions of dollars of new revenue. All I received was a small payment to achieve a huge undertaking. Was it worth it for me? Would I ever do this again? Never!

All of this was chalked up as experience of being used and exploited. I came to the conclusion that after I achieved the level the company wanted I was no longer an asset to them. So, I packed up and moved south to another city, to a new life. So do I believe there is a guarantee in being an employee? I don't see any especially after this experience. My beliefs were completely shattered and in the end, it changed another part of my beliefs and my employee mind-set.

All I know about the people that did this to me is...

Karma's a bitch!

DON'T MOVE

Yes, don't move, hop or bounce around please. You should stay put. Well you may be a bit confused, and wondering what it is I am talking about. The point I am raising here is about aggressive and ambitious employees who are looking for more. These individuals are searching for opportunities like a better job, higher pay, more benefits, better working conditions and a clear path to excel. An employee wanting to improve their status and livelihood is a positive action. However, it isn't a benefit for companies when their employees leave.

Companies focus on employee retention for a number of reasons which are both monetary and intangible. This is why changing employers becomes a disadvantage for employees. Employers want to retain them because of the costs associated with bringing a new hire up to a point of being productive and adding value to the company. This is a big investment for the company that includes HR or agency costs, advertising, interviewing, screening and finally hiring the right candidate and onboarding. Then after hiring, the company continues to provide more training and manage the candidate.

The training and management period can be anywhere from 6 months to 2 years before a new hire's productivity is comparable to that of an existing employee. The monetary costs are up to two years of salary plus any additional training costs over a 24 month period which average at least 25% of their yearly salary.

There are other factors that play a role for employees who stay long term at companies. Employees actually become assets that appreciate, gaining more and more value the longer they stay. The reason being, long term employees reach a sound understanding of the company's big picture. Their experience and knowledge about the company's products and services enhance the company's customer service, reputation, products, services, quality and so on.

Besides the monetary costs of employees who leave, there are other subtle things that make negative impacts which can affect other employees, especially if the employee is unhappy before leaving. A negative attitude can affect and sway the overall morale of many employees, and reduce productivity, since all it takes is one bad apple.

As a result, employers frown upon individuals that frequently change companies because of the monetary and intangible losses. So when companies review a resume or CV that shows a potential candidate is switching jobs frequently, this clearly suggests the individual is inconsistent and unstable. This observation immediately brings up a flag with many concerns and questions, such as,

1. "If we hire this person, how long are they going to stay with our company? It looks like they change companies every six months, then we have to start the whole process all over again."

2. "Do we want to hire someone who has had 7 jobs in the past five years? This candidate is too much of a risk for our organization since it appears they have no loyalty or stability."

3. "Is this person just going to get some experience and training then go to one of our competitors shortly after for more money? It sure looks like it according to the salary history this person provided."

4. "Think of the costs of time, effort and training it takes to bring a new hire to a productive level. This person will leave at that point, and then we start all over again. Who else is there that we can consider other than this candidate?"

5. "Next, forget this candidate lets hire someone who wants to stay long term and climb our career ladder"

Generally, companies are looking to hire employees who are loyal, stable and consistent who are willing to stay for the long haul. The basic stereotype of stable people that companies are looking for includes individuals who are experienced, mature, married, and have a family.

For example, I was always searching for new jobs. When looking over my resume or CV the employers could clearly see that I would stay in positions for 6 to 36 months then move on. This was clearly a sign of instability and on several occasions I was asked directly, why they should hire me when I am switching jobs all the time.

All I could say was that, I was interested in their position, required work to earn a living and discussed some of the problems and reasons why I had left some past employers. At times, this was enough for many companies but some employers would outright not hire me based on my pattern of jumping from job to job and company to company. However, I felt I had just cause for hopping around and besides I had many reasons not excuses.

As far as the reasons that were propelling me to hop around from company to company all stemmed from details like:

- Being bored
- No path for advancement
- No new opportunities
- No new interests
- No structure or policies in place
- Too much travel
- Completely disorganized company
- Too much overtime

- High stress and anxiety
- Change of the management and management style
- Change of environment
- Company values and my values not aligned
- Poor economic conditions or factors
- Unfair treatment
- Personal problems that arose while employed, that could not be dealt with while employed such as loss of loved one, relationship problems and so on
- Fit at first and after some time didn't fit anymore
- Not fun or interesting anymore
- Have plateaued in knowledge
- Not enough money
- Found better paying jobs
- No salary increases
- Information in interview before taking the job was not the truth

- Many people upset, angry, with very low morale

- Your expectations and their expectations do not align

- Conflict with other coworkers due to coworkers viewing me as a threat instead of a team player

I found the primary reasons for hopping around are generally because of a few main reasons like, the job is a dead end as far as career advancement goes, low wages, not fitting in anymore which is based on values, policies, principles, expectations and so on. The best one and my all-time favorite is what you were told in the interview prior to accepting the job, is totally different from what it really is. This includes, work environment, morale of employees, treatment and other things. This reminds me of an example of having ethics problems with a company.

For example, when I was working for a large electrical company, as an industrial electronics technologist, I was paid well, had a company car and would do service calls around the city on anything that had electronics, like a furnace used for heat treating Boeing aircraft parts, optical coating machines, electroplating machines, or Faulkner F-28 airplane ground power supply units.

The company was privately owned and the president of the company was a blunt, aloof, insensitive, impersonal, money oriented, serious, and cheap person. He lived without any feelings so people were treated accordingly. I didn't know this at the time since I very rarely had any dealings with this person. However, the reason I did find these things out about him was, the situation I heard and witnessed when standing three feet from the conversations.

On this day an employee Gary was an inside sale person for the company for two decades and a really nice fellow. He had a bubbly personality and was quite entertaining. However, I remember him entering the electronics lab, and looked very uncomfortable and holding his abdomen as if he was in deep pain. He blurted out to Allan a senior tech, "Al, you have to drive me to the hospital, there is something seriously wrong with me, because I'm in so much bloody pain!" Allan, immediately told Gary he would do it immediately. So, they left the shop and I…was quite concerned about Gary.

About 15 minutes later the owner came into the lab and asked, "Does anyone know where Allan is?" then James replied, "Allan drove Gary to the hospital emergency and it looked like Gary was in deep pain with some serious problem." The owner didn't say anything he just walked out.

About two hours later, Allan returned without Gary. I asked, "Allan is Gary okay, what happened? Allan replied, "He had some abdominal problems and went straight into exploratory surgery!" I replied, "Oh wow sounds really serious I sure hope he is okay". Alan said," No worries, he is in good hands, I'm sure they will find out what it is." About 10 minutes later the owner walks in and approaches Allan. The owner immediately asks, "Allan where were you?" and Allen responded, "I drove Gary to the closest Hospital Emergency because he was having some serious problem". The owner coldly replied, "Allan don't ever do that kind of stuff like that again, because you know that we have cheaper labor in the back shop that could have drove him!"

I was about three feet away from the conversation and couldn't believe my ears; it was as if this person wasn't human. Not one molecule of compassion or empathy, I was disgusted, at the thought of working for this cold-hearted a-hole. I stood there thinking about what I wanted to say and it would have sounded something like this, "Just wait you frickin a-hole until you have a heart-attack and I'll be sure to throw you a quarter so you can call yourself a taxi! " Of course I didn't say anything. Shortly after though, I found a job with another company and left immediately, because I couldn't work for someone like this.

Regardless of the reasons, an employee hopping around frequently puts the employee at a disadvantage, because many companies will immediately overlook their resume. Some companies may call you in for an interview because of your experience and to get a feel about your intentions and mindset, but overall they are leery about hiring you.

Other companies may hire you then you leave shortly after, because you will find out the true realities of the company and the environment. In other words, it's like a sweat shop and they should have a revolving front door because of such high employee turnover. As long as you are an employee, and you have many job transitions on your resume and keep jumping around, you are at a full disadvantage.

BENEFITS PACKAGE

I feel that benefits packages are more hype and disadvantages than a benefit. I say this because the reality is benefits are not free. Each employee must pay for their benefits package coverage via monthly deductions off their paycheck.

Another point is geared towards the employee benefits being mandatory. This means that the employee has no choice regardless if they want them or not. So the employee has no choice to choose what benefits or coverage they would like or what insurance company will provide them.

Also, there are restrictions and limitations your benefits provider places on how much you actually can claim on each item of your benefits package. Some examples are vision care, psychological services, physio therapy, massage therapy and so on. Generally benefits coverage is only a fraction of the total cost, usually 20 to 25% and limited to a yearly total claim amount except prescription drugs which have 90% coverage. For example, when using the massage benefit, a one hour massage may cost

$90 and the benefits plan will cover $20 of the cost for a total of 12 sessions or $240 per year. Therefore, as an employee, you pay $70 out of pocket per massage. If we look at the costs over a year, benefits pay $240 for 12 sessions while the employee out of pocket expense is $840.

When claiming other benefits, such as dental expenses, there is always a waiting period of 3 months before the benefit is active. Additionally, there are set limits of coverage for crowns, dentures, regular check-ups and cleaning services. For example, the insurance company covers only 50% of the crowns costs and there are also limitations on the yearly claim amount.

In other words, to have a crown installed may cost $1,500 but after benefits are applied, this is reduced to $750 for the employee's out of pocket costs. However, if you add in a cleaning and a checkup, you may have reached the yearly limit for dental coverage. What if you need another crown and you want to use your dental coverage, but have already reached the maximum yearly claim amount. Now you may have to wait until the next year to have the crown work done. Basically, the insurance company is dictating when you will get your dental work done and covered.

What if you can't wait and you need dental work now? The employee will pay out of pocket costs for the full amount. When paying out of pocket dental expenses, only a small portion of the total cost is allowed to be used as a claim on your income tax return. For example, in Canada if the medical expenses you and your family are claiming are eligible according to the CRA, you can claim up to 3% of your total income or $2,208 whichever is lower. Also keep in mind that the CRA, HMRC and IRS have a list of eligible expenses that can be claimed. Note that the total claim amount on the income tax form is not a direct deduction only a fixed and small percentage of it.

Another point to add is the insurance company benefits provider is not going to allow employees to claim amounts that surpass the employee's yearly benefit contribution amount because the insurance company has to make money too. If benefit contributions are being exceeded by the amount employees claim then benefits costs will rise.

This is only a basic example of why benefits are not really a benefit because the amount the employee contributes to the benefit plan is equal to or more than the amount the plan covers. As an employee you are paying out of pocket medical type expenses for most items with NET income which has already been taxed.

GOVERNMENT PENSION CONTRIBUTIONS

Pension contributions for government based pension plans are a disadvantage since there is no real guarantee the funds will exist in the future. Besides, who can make predictions of 30 or 40 years into the future? No one can predict the future only make estimates which are neither correct nor reliable. I feel that many employees can be paying into something that may not even exist by the time they actually need the funds. The payments being made for pension plans or social security are deducted from each employee's paycheck and are mandatory, with no choice to opt out even if employees want to. There is more information about this topic that I cover later on in the text.

CHANGES IN THE WORKPLACE

Changes in the workplace always occur and they are inevitable because of technology advancements, competition, leadership shuffles, strategy changes, economic turbulence, and market forces and so on. Changes are made at many different levels; some are minor like process changes while others are substantial like policy or leadership changes. These kinds of major changes of course impact every employee. The most drastic changes I have seen is, when a leadership shuffle occurs and new senior management appointments are made throughout the company.

This is an eye-opener since with new leadership in place, immediately new leaders have to prove their existence, start making drastic changes, appointing VPs to other sectors of the company and those VPs appoint new managers and so on down the hierarchy. Most importantly, the changes in an organization like leadership, usually introduces a different culture and environment. With changes like this, employees have no control or choice in these matters other than to wait and see what the outcome is.

So this means that if you were fitting in before enjoying your job, you may soon find out you do not fit in the new culture and environment anymore. This in fact is the uncomfortable part of this type of change since; the employee may become frustrated with the changes, because they may have lost their existing position, or have been relieved of their management duties to now have to report to a new manager. Now the demeanor of the newly assigned manager leading the department may immediately provoke employees to seek transfers to other departments within the company just for their own sanity, or if possible attempt to work for their old manager if they are still employed.

This situation presents a huge disruption and risk for an employee that has set their sights on long-term security, comfort and pension. Furthermore, maybe management will phase out the employees job and others, downsize the union workforce, so the employee may eventually not even have a job after giving the company many years of service already.

Changes can have the potential to abruptly upset the apple cart in the workplace and most importantly, current long term employees have to change their attitude and views in order to cope with new management or the company changes. If the employees don't change, they may be left with being unhappy, eventually losing morale and leaving the workplace, resulting in giving up pension, seniority and years of service. I feel that this is definitely a disadvantage.

GOING SOLO

Another employee disadvantage I found was not having the ability to go solo by starting a business. Being employed by a company the employee is obligated to perform services and tasks that are all based on their qualifications and background. With that in mind, an employee must work for the company exclusively and cannot hire other employees to increase their own salary or pay. However, even if the employee decides to open a business like a sole proprietorship on the side, this may pose as a conflict of interest with the employer, which is a breach of the employment or union agreements.

With a conflict of interest, the employee could possibly lose their job or immediately be forced to close their little company. If the employee opens a sole proprietorship successfully to make some extra money, to launch themselves into doing something new and stimulating, or to eventually be able to quit their current job may not be possible. Why? It all sounds great in theory but most of the time it doesn't really bare any fruit.

I say this because I've tried this several times myself. I found that I was lacking resources, time, and money since there was too much of an obligation to fulfil my primary function that was the main source of income I was living on. So, after plugging away, I very rarely found the time and energy to make a lift off with my own company. Then again, keep in mind the powers at hand like the CRA, HMRC, or IRS only give you so much time with a business to make a profit but only showing company losses. The company losses are usually start-up expenses you have accumulated for your small business venture.

Of course, I'm not telling you not to embark on a sole proprietorship adventure. Just because I couldn't seem to get one off the ground doesn't mean that you can't. In fact, it may end up being the most successful venture in your entire life. With that in mind, you will have to take a leap, join the contractor-corporations and may have to leave the security of being an employee.

I just want everyone to be prosperous and successful at any venture. However, most are too scared to, don't have the time, resources, and may risk their current job in the process. Besides, in order to get a business off the ground requires more time that an employee has available which poses as another disadvantage.

DEFINED HOLIDAYS

When it comes to employee holidays things are great, you go on holidays and you get paid the whole time you are gone. The disadvantage I have found is holidays are dictated by the company and their policies. Some of the common policies assign the length of allowable holidays based on employee years of service. Holiday time is commonly incremented at intervals of 5, 10 and 20 years of service. This allowable time off is also governed by labor standards or law. So, when companies are developing a policy for employee holidays they must at minimum meet or exceed labor standards for federal, provincial, or state regions.

Examples of some typical holiday periods in North America are:

- 1 to 5 years of service provides 2 or 3 weeks

- 5 to 10 years of service provides 3 to 4 weeks

- 15 years of service provides 4 to 5 weeks

- 20 years of service provides 5 to 6 weeks

When taking into account each company's policies, holiday lengths will be different, based on, the country, state, province or region you reside in. These holiday periods, are decided by law and by the union or non-union company you work for and not the employee.

Another point about holidays is in respect to union and non-union companies. In a non-unionized company, the employees must submit their proposed holiday time to their supervisor or manager, so the manager can decide whether or not the employees can take their holidays in that time period. This decision is based on, the holiday fitting into the overall work schedule or if there is a conflict. Work always takes precedence over holidays.

Unionized companies use a timetable for allotting holiday days. However, the employees choose holiday periods in a chronological order based on years of service or levels of seniority. This is another disadvantage to take into account. For instance, when working within a unionized company, the employee with the most seniority has first choice of when and how many of their holidays they will use and so on. This process continues down the seniority list until the last level of seniority personnel is reached. Usually at this point there is no ideal time period left. So, if you are at the low end of the seniority list forget that wonderful camping trip you had planned in July since it probably won't be available. Instead you will be freezing your ass off camping in November or December.

I remember this union seniority cluster very well. I was at the bottom of the seniority list and when I finally got to pick my holidays, and the only choice I had was November. Yes, in November I was freezing my ass off camping.

PIGEON HOLED

Being pigeon holed is a huge disadvantage since any employee can be pigeon holed and be held in their current position. The employee may be doing their professional best with high efficiency and productivity in order to progress into another position only later to be disappointed. The reason is, the employee does an excellent job at their current position and their collective performance is exactly what helps that team and department do a great job.

For instance, if the manager allows the employee to take-on a different position, they may not be able to find a trustworthy replacement that will do the same level of job the previous employee was doing. In other words, the employee is not going anywhere because of their great performance.

Another reason for this pigeon holing could be a silent bias against the employee that management may have, thus denying the employee to climb the company ladder to new heights while others are allowed to advance. To add to this bias, I have found that several companies only remember employee mistakes or errors and disregard any of the positive contributions and successes the employee has made.

These negative actions taken by the company directly affect the employee's morale, loyalty, belief, enthusiasm and hope. In fact, the employees have placed themselves in a dead end career without even knowing it. Unfortunately this forces the employee to seek an opportunity elsewhere even though they were true long-term employees. Do you remember what the result of changing jobs too many times is?

EXPENSE ACCOUNTS

Another item I found was the use of an expense account and having to, in most circumstances, put up my own money to cover the company as far as expenses were concerned. Using my own credit card was okay for small purchases but when purchasing items with my own credit card; management would review the purchases then remove or not cover certain purchases based on the company's disapproval or even their own biased disapproval.

In other words, I would use my own money to purchase items that were required for doing the field work, but the company wouldn't reimburse the purchase. So I was unhappy with using my credit card when having purchases scrutinized and the manager deciding what the company pays and doesn't pay. At times, I was left holding hundreds of dollars of unpaid credit card balance because the purchases were not allowed.

On other occasions, I received a corporate credit card. While using the corporate credit card, it was restricted to only cover certain items while, the need for other items couldn't be purchased. When covering the company with my own credit card or cash, the company accounting process would take long to reimburse that would incur interest rate charges on my credit card. Of course I would have to tally up the interest for payment then resubmit.

This whole process was quite frustrating. Even when using the corporate credit card, the items purchased would be scrutinized and I would owe the company for items I purchased for work, because they were not covered. So, regardless of my personal or corporate credit card, I was always getting hit with "out of pocket" expenses. I got to a point of asking for an itemized list of things that were allowed because it was too subjective.

For instance, when travelling to international work locations some field based circumstances, would max out my credit card at $50,000. I would carry the balance until the company paid the credit card. In this kind of situation the risk was very high because if the company became financially unstable or insolvent, they would leave me with the credit card bill of $50,000 to pay. I truly felt uncomfortable with carrying such large balances and debt risk especially on my own credit card.

You may be sitting there thinking that there is no risk because the company has to pay my credit card bill. Sure, but keep in mind when you are working for a company, and they become insolvent or go into receivership or bankruptcy, you won't know it until it's too late. In bankruptcy or insolvency, the money that the company has, first will go to all main credit holders.

The legal entity in charge of the bankruptcy litigation will go through the list of creditors paying each one, starting from the top which is usually banks. After they finally reach you at the very bottom of the list, they tell you there is nothing left. Consequently, you are stuck paying a company credit card bill personally. Sounds like a wonderful situation to be a part of, don't you think?

Now that we have covered what I feel are employee disadvantages, there are a few things that employees should know about, like, some of the false hopes and beliefs that employees generally have, which are controlling employee's lives every day.

Page Left Blank

THE SECRETS

In this section we look at some of the secret truths behind what some employees believe about such topics as, job security, blame, false security, climbing a corporate ladder, employee benefits packages, and pensions.

Hopefully, this will shed some insight and awareness about these topics to help open up a different perspective to think about. In fact, many employees hold these false beliefs close to heart that influence their lives and decisions.

MISSION STATEMENTS

Mission statements are written by employees and senior executive management that are about the organization or company. The mission statement defines why the company or organization exists, who their main customers or clients are, and what the company wants to achieve. Ideally, a mission statement provides the company and organization with direction, ensures decision making is in alignment to stay on course; and provides a clear purpose so business strategies can be focused on achieving the company's business goals.

However, the drawbacks to mission statements are usually unreachable, and cannot be fulfilled by the company and the organization. Additionally, if the mission statement is unreasonable, then the company may make skewed decisions based on reaching the unsound mission goal which in fact is unfavorable and damaging to the company and its future.

To further support this notion of mission statements, they are printed on fancy paper then placed in high quality frames and displayed on the walls around the company. This display of the statement is to demonstrate to employees that the organization supports goals and to remind them of this.

However, in over thirty years of being employed, I have yet to find one company that actually can stand behind their mission statement or attain it. I say this since it's all a load of hoo-ha and their actions tell the truth. I have found that many mission statements are only words with no real substance or truth.

POLICIES AND PROCEDURES

Policies and procedures of a company are created to document any company actions, activities and choices. These are all carried out within the set boundaries and limits the organization has designed. All policies and procedures impact all employees of the organization.

Company policies are written to indoctrinate their rules, beliefs, boundaries, standards and guidelines in order to reach their long term objectives. These policies are published and available to all employees. Furthermore, HR training sessions are provided for all employees in regard to the organization's policies and ethics.

Company procedures are developed to support the organization's policies. Procedures capture step-by-step methods in order to create repeatable practices within the company that are used during daily operations. Employees are trained to instill awareness and teach procedural practices used by the organization.

Again, in over thirty years of employment, I have yet to find one company that actually conforms to their own policies, and procedures. Most polices are just words with no corresponding action deeming them as worthless. In truth, I found many of the company policies and even some standards and procedures are sadly enough, overridden by management's egotism, favoritism and power.

THE BLAME GAME

Another popular false truth that I have found amongst employees is blaming the company or their employer. The employee's attitudes and beliefs make them blame the employer for their own personal financial situation. The blame stems from the employee holding a certain position in the company and receiving a corresponding salary. However, as time passes they start to accumulate debt, make purchases and establish a certain level of lifestyle. Unknown to the employee is that they are living beyond their means or affordability. The spending for an elevated lifestyle continues until, the true financial situation comes to the forefront.

The reality strikes the employee and starts to feel that money is becoming scarcer. This means that shortly after being paid, the employee has less and less cash in their pocket. This is considered as a financial warning sign or pinch that the employee usually ignores. Nonetheless, the employee continues with spending and other habits with no change. About six months after the initial pinch, suddenly everything all at once seems to come to a screeching halt. This is what I call the financial squeeze and the current financial reality coming to the forefront. This is when the employee starts to feel the real pain related to the financial conditions brought on by the employee's own desire to live a better life style. This is in fact when the employee has no cash except to look at bills and make decisions to choose which bill to skip, in order to maintain cash in hand and spending.

The employee at this point begins to ask questions about the situation like, why don't I have any money? Why did this happen? Is my rent too high? Did my car insurance increase? Where is all my money going? The answers are quite simple, since it is the employee that has exclusively created the financial mess. Their answer to the situation is that they are not being paid enough. With this deduction, the employee goes to the boss to ask for a raise. The result is the employee finds out they are being paid the maximum amount for their current position. The refusal of having a raise makes the employee frustrated and upset. Since now the financial pressures and pain, as well as, the rejection of getting a raise, together change the attitude of the employee. To protect their own feelings and dignity they start to blame the company or the employer for not paying enough and start looking for another job.

The reality with these kinds of situations is this: The employer has a number of positions within the company that all have corresponding salary ranges. Each salary range is calculated to ensure it is cost effective and aligned with salary benchmarks for the specific industry. This allows the company to not only be competitive with paying salaries to their employees but also enables the company to remain being profitable and a competitive business. In other words, there are salary limitations for any position in any company even though employees don't understand this nor want to.

They in turn would rather blame the company instead, of facing the errors they have made with their own finances. The employee feels it's the company's fault that they have financial problems which is false. There is only so much money an employee can get paid regardless of their occupation whether they are a, technician, auto mechanic, document manager, doctor, accountant, senior manager, plumber, carpenter, cost engineer, design engineer, welder, senior manager, CEO, VP, admin support, IT professional, and so on. There is always a hierarchy for positions, pay scale and the return on investment of each position. *This means that pay is calculated based on how much financial impact the position has on the company.*

For instance, a manager gets paid more than their subordinates because of their skill sets, training, responsibilities, education, experience, competencies and the overall impact the position has within the company. Another angle is a company's research and development (R &D) department and employees are like a money pit. The R&D requires large amounts of resources and money without directly providing an actual return on the investment. However this group is essential for the company's innovations, competitive edge and future, which in the end provides an intangible return on investment. In fact, without the R&D department the company's future would be short lived.

So the employee blaming the company is not realistic. The truth lies in self-reflection to see what the problem is and what is causing their financial problems. Also, if they want to increase their salary to elevate their lifestyle and quality of life, they must first increase their education, training, skill sets, experience, and competencies.

CAREER ADVANCEMENT

Many employees believe they have the ability and a clear pathway to climb the corporate ladder, and to get a better paying position. Employees think that there is opportunity for everyone and that any employee can climb the ladder if they choose to. This may be true but the reality is that some management will use favoritism, bias, grudges and power to bypass them from advancing. In other words not all employees are eligible for career advancements even though they may qualify more so than others. Another downside of career advancement is when employees are self-centered, power hungry and egotistical. They are only geared and driven to advance themselves and don't care what they have to do to get there. People with this kind of attitude, only introduce egotism, back stabbing, favoritism, humiliation, discrimination, and other related negative behaviors into the workplace. This is all for their personal power and gain, with no regard, for anyone else.

Of course, these types of behaviors only make the workplace an undesirable and unpleasant place to work because many people get hurt on both professional and personal levels. These go-getter cut throats that have no conscience, really don't give two shits about co-workers, their wellbeing only themselves. When egotistical types like this make it to management, they, because of the abrasive demeanor, immediately lose many of their subordinates who are in fact excellent employees.

Throughout my twenties and part of my thirties I was driven as well but, never pissed people off, stepped on their toes, wasn't a cutthroat, or a bully. For instance, when I started at my first real career industry job, I worked long hours and studied hard to learn about the equipment I was working with. This was all so I could achieve and move from a trainee position to a junior level position. I achieved the junior level within 7 months while the average timeframe was 12 to 18 months.

Furthermore, I was able to show and convince upper management of my abilities and knowledge. This allowed me to enter the bidding for a Middle East technical advisor position only after 2 ½ years of employment. Usually the bidding process consisted of senior employees which have 7 to 10 years of experience. In fact senior candidates could take any opportunity they wanted to, reducing my chances to almost zero except for this one. Many candidates hesitated to apply because the position was in an unstable and precarious region of the world.

This position was located in Ahwaz, Iran, a highly volatile place just six months after the eight year Iran–Iraq war was halted. There was no peace or war declared and everything was in limbo. In fact, there were over 500,000 Iraqi soldiers still lined up along the border. I was afraid, but it didn't deter me because I was determined and driven to become a specialist, a technical advisor in the Middle East.

I played the odds anyway, and was the first candidate to apply for the position. I acted on the premise of probability, meaning other people's fears being greater than my own. I also found that most of the senior candidates were married with children and speculated that they wouldn't take a risk. While I on the other hand, felt that I was a prime candidate being single, with no ties and ready to go. Based on all of my assumptions, I knew this would be my only chance to work in an international location.

In the end my assumptions were correct, I won the bidding since no one else wanted to go but one other person who became my shift relief. Besides being a technical advisor, I wanted to see and experience another country being adventurous in my mid-twenties and I never stepped foot into a foreign country before. Consequently, after winning the bid, my first country travelled was going to be Iran or how the locals would call it "*Eron.*"

Before embarking on the journey, I didn't research Iran like others on the crew; I on the other hand was more interested in speaking to the Iranians directly. All I remember throughout my childhood adolescents was that Iran and Iraq did this and that, and was unstable. I didn't ever really understand what the whole fight was between Iran and Iraq. It was absolutely something that I could never imagine until I arrived there.

Upon arrival, I realized the work location was situated in a war zone only 40 miles from the Iraqi border. In fact the Iraqis came within 3 miles from Ahwaz. This city became a safe haven for migrant refugees that came from the war torn surrounding communities and a main border city, called Abadan. According to the locals, Abadan had universities and was a thriving city that unfortunately was destroyed and didn't exist anymore.

Now, Ahwaz was a city of over 2 million people, with electrical power continuously load shedding, buildings blown apart into rubble, many injured, and with countless people mourning for their lost loved ones. Shockingly many people I spoke to had lost 8 to 10 family members during the war. It was truly unfortunate, painful and heartbreaking for those innocent families and people. To me it was horrifying, disturbing, and laborious. I could not relate to this harsh reality especially coming from North America where there is no war and people are driven by money and excelling at their careers.

During my twenties to my mid-thirties I had the drive to succeed, excel and get to the top, climb a mountain, and of course, had that invincible, "I'll be president one day" kind of attitude. After so many years of succeeding at climbing the ladders and taking on roles of field supervisor, technical manager, training manager, technical advisor, and project manager, I realized that all this hype about management positions in my opinion… wasn't worth it.

In management or supervisory roles, you are expected to take full responsibility, put in extra hours and effort to do whatever it takes. If you recall my technical manager story, all of the worries, stress, anxiety and extra time were shortening my lifespan, and in the end it was never really worth the extra money. All of these things only add pressure and stress that weakens our immune system and induces physical illness, such as irritable bowel, high blood pressure, acid reflux, ulcers, nervous conditions, and creates insomnia. Then we have to find ways to cope with these conditions of anxiety, tensions and worries.

To cope with the added pressures and stress some people turn to smoking, drinking and drugs, while others use exercise and a fitness routine. Many people also resort to their physician prescribing medications for depression, anxiety and panic such as, Prozac, Paxil, Zoloft or other serotonin-reuptake-inhibitor medications (SSRIs). So, is management for you or worth it?

What I found was that the higher and higher you climb the ladder the responsibilities and stress increase proportionally. In truth this all added up to months and years of my personal time gone. This was time I had lost that I will never get back, ever. Sorry, but after all of the management experiences I've had; I'd rather make a couple of bucks less per hour and go home at 5 pm every night, so I can relax, and enjoy my personal time. As far as I am concerned, let others worry about it and have the stress for the extra bucks because…life is just too short.

JOB GUARANTEES

As far as job security goes, having a job without ever losing it… well it doesn't exist, because anyone can lose their job at the drop of a hat regardless; whether you are a laborer, supervisor, senior manager, VP, director or even CEO. Generally, in some circumstances job loss can happen quickly, while in other situations it is tardy. Most importantly it "can" happen; and I have seen and experienced it.

As any employee, even if you are fired or let go, there is at most times, a severance package, and employment insurance benefits to fall back on. Even if there isn't a package, it may cost the company 20, or 30 or even 50 grand but who cares, you are still out of a job. Then, you have to pay tax on the money they give you, and if it's a wrongful dismissal you also pay your lawyer to win a lawsuit.

If we also add in economic or market forces, such as, commodity market free fall just like oil in the past couple of years has fallen from $150 per barrel to below $30. This itself creates havoc on the job front as well as impacting any commodity based economies like, Saudi, Qatar, Kuwait, USA, Canada, Norway, UK and many others causing slow growth and high unemployment. This only proves that, no one or any company is immune to deep economic impact since it affects all industries anywhere in the world.

However, some employees are oblivious to market impacts, believing nothing will happen and place their trust in their employer. They believe that the company will continue to prosper regardless of the economic conditions. Of course many companies do weather such storms and survive the economic turmoil but do not remain unscathed. Keep in mind that the largest cost and expense for a company is always the employee payroll.

For example, just recently, Hewlett Packard announced that it was cutting 30,000 employees. If we do a quick calculation and crunch some numbers, it gives us a clearer picture of why their decision was to let go 30,000 employees. Generally, if each employee's average salary was $36,000 a year or $3000 a month that would equate to a savings of $90 million per month or $1.08 billion a year not including the cost of the employee benefits packages. With benefit packages this would add an additional 30 percent or $27 million a month or $324 million a year.

Another item to add stems from employees thinking they have a guaranteed job, especially those in unions, which is never the case. Many employees believe they will never get fired or laid-off and nothing will ever change. The employees also believe that even if the economy faces huge commodity downturns like in the oil industry they will be untouched. Guess again. For example, the oil sands, in Canada, alone were hit very hard and job losses were happening by the tens of thousands, including those in unions. Moreover, in the US, the situation wasn't much different. In Canada the total job loss so far according to an August 31, 2015, CBC article is 35,000 to date.

This article is found at the following URL:

http://www.cbc.ca/news/business/alberta-has-lost-35-000-oilpatch-jobs-petroleum-producers-say-1.3208717

According to the April 14, 2015, Wall Street Journal article, over 100,000 oil workers worldwide have lost their jobs, so far. The full article can be found at the following URL:

http://www.wsj.com/articles/oil-layoffs-hit-100-000-and-counting-1429055740

The whole belief about being guaranteed has no bearing or truth since all of us on the whole, have no guarantee in anything in our lives. Moreover, especially what a company decides. Companies are doing whatever is necessary to please shareholders, to endure economic forces, like layoffs, and program cuts, and some companies will even merge in order to survive.

Throughout my experiences, I have seen many situations of high unemployment when people lose their jobs, such as, directors, VPs, CEOs, laborers, engineers, sales people, and others. I have taken a reduction in pay, taken time off with no pay, to accommodate my employer. I have also outright lost jobs, because of economic or commodity market downturns.

In reality, there is no such thing as job security since to have full and complete security, would mean that there would be no risk. In truth though, risk can only be reduced and minimized, not eliminated. Therefore, risks always exist and with it job security risks. However, in order to improve your chances of having more job security than others is to be flexible even if it means taking pay cuts, time off and other measures the company feels are necessary.

FALSE SENSE OF SECURITY

Some privately owned companies are still doing business by pushing paper unlike the big kids on the block that have elaborate and innovative systems. Not all companies are at a high tech stage nor do they want to be. The reason is, there is no need because, things seem to be running smoothly, they are still in business, making a profit and the employees have been working there forever.

With that in mind, the company has employees that have been there for over 20 to 30 years or more and know everything to do with the company and their processes. Within these companies there has never been a real need for formal documentation only a few informal documents that are used. Therefore, there have never been any recorded or documented policies, processes, manuals, work instructions, procedures, and guidelines to support the company or new or existing employees. Instead the company relies on the long term senior employee's knowledge, experience and subjectivity.

These senior employees are considered by many as old school. These individuals believe that the knowledge they carry in their head, is their job security, meaning that they will never get fired or let go. This in reality is a false sense of security especially with today's technologies, and educated workforce. Anyone can be replaced at any time, regardless of their extensive experience, knowledge or position they retain. When employees believe that retaining information will prevent them from being fired, laid-off or replaced, it is in truth, all false.

Even if the company lost the individuals who retain all the knowledge, other people can replace those people, which may cause only temporary delays and setbacks for the company. However, the company moves forward regardless of who quits, dies, or leaves. Companies have established a customer base over their lifetime of business that has generated millions of dollars of income, each and every year and that continues on year after year.

A company's whole function, or products, services or whatever they do, does not all stand because of one person or a couple of people. For instance, the owner and founder of Microsoft had some visionary gifts, yet, there are always others who exist in the world or even within the company that have similar or even superior vision.

Consequently, every company does require leadership. However, the company is in business because of all of the company employees combined carrying out each function and all of the tasks to implement the leadership ideas. Together, this is what makes the company successful and what they are today and beyond.

PENSION MY ASS

The Magical Day

I discussed pensions in an earlier section however this section covers a few different viewpoints about pension. While working for many companies, especially unionized ones, I discovered many employees were focused on retirement. They were waiting to reach a magical age of 65, and were just counting the days until they retire.

Meanwhile, these same employees dread getting up every morning, day after day, year after year and going into a workplace they despise. Most importantly, they are unaware that as they continue towards retirement they are actually working themselves into the grave due to the stress. To support this view, according to the October 10th, 2013 Forbes article called, "Unhappy Employees Outnumber Happy Ones by Two to One Worldwide" which states that; "there are twice as many workers that hate their job than those who love their job." In fact, many people would leave their job in a second if they had the courage and confidence or the money. Consequently, many are stuck in the same rut until retirement regardless of their true wishes.

I also learned that many employees' main focus was to wait for retirement; these employees sit at home, save their money, and refrain from pursuing things they like to do and enjoy. Their main excuse for denying themselves was they could do these things at retirement. Some of the things they would put on hold were travel, painting, writing, art, gardening, singing, playing piano, second language, dancing and other activities. Consequently, these employees place their lives on hold until their magical retirement age of sixty five and then they start living.

Many people don't realize that as we continue to age, we change mentally and physically throughout the aging cycle. Our biological changes all affect our skin, bones, joints, muscles, body shape, our looks, teeth and gums, hair and nails, immune system, memory, hearing, vision, smell and taste, bowel and bladder function, as well as, sleep patterns. Hey is there anything that I left out? Seriously, these things change regardless of our inadequate diets or our vices.

Even with all these age related changes occurring many of us keep doing the same things as we did in our youth. With that in mind, many individuals health starts to deteriorate because of their, continued use of alcohol, cigarettes, drugs, illegal or OTC. For instance, according to the world health organization (WHO) over 80% of the world's 1 billion smokers live in low to middle income countries. Tobacco at minimum kills at least 50% of its users.

To add to this most of us have an unhealthy diet and poor eating habits. Many of us are unaware of our metabolic changes which make us gain weight very rapidly that may lead to obesity and diabetes. This change usually begins in our forties and weight gain is so quick, in fact, just by looking at a box of cookies you can immediately feel your ass grow! On top of it all, many of us also don't exercise which is a main ingredient to combat the effects of aging.

So, if you add all of this up it's a perfect formula for serious health problems in our later years. According to some surveys those with poor health before retirement generally only live about 18 months after retirement. It has also been found that early retirement at 55 compared to 65 equates to earlier death too.

Putting life on hold and waiting until retirement, isn't reasonable at all. I stress this since; as we get older many of us are not as energetic, mobile, flexible, and agile, as we were during our youthful years. Even though we still can maintain physical fitness and retain muscle mass just like we had in our thirties. Waiting a long time for something in life isn't living, since with life, we just never know what lies ahead like, serious illness, accidents, arthritis, heart problems, stroke, hip replacement, vision impairment or loss, heart attack, high blood pressure, glaucoma, diabetes, obesity, or other diseases and even sudden death.

So living today, at least allows us to live each day, to do things we like and enjoy without depriving ourselves which doesn't require retirement. We can do it today, retired or not and live that passion out while we still have our youth, mobility and health. There is nothing in this world to stop you from learning pottery, dancing, painting, art, writing, piano, gardening and so on… except you.

When we live in the "now", we are living day by day, enjoying each day as they pass. Waiting for something of course can have exceptions. For example, when I was working at this company, I remember being in a conversation with a couple of co-workers. We got on the topic of lotteries. One of the workers immediately piped up and said, "If I won the lottery, I would go shit right on top of the director's desk!" and then I asked, "Why wait until you win the lottery?"

For quite a while now over two decades, I have lost confidence in predicting the future and stopped living in fear and anxiety worried about retirement and the magical day in my life. I decided to join, not the freedom 55 plan but the freedom 90 plan instead.

Pension Ya Right

Many people are employees mainly because of the bright light at the end of the tunnel called pension. In many people's minds, government or company based pensions or even their own pension savings are full proof because these funds will be there when employees retire. For the fortunate ones, yes there will be a pension plan or a retirement savings account with funds. However, many people still ask which kind of plan is the better one to have.

The most popular company pension plans involve two types which are a "defined benefit" and a "defined contribution" pension scheme. A defined benefit pension plan is when the company guarantees a pension income for each employee at the end of their service. The amount of the pension payment is derived by using a set of metrics. These metrics are based on, the years of being a member of the plan, the employee's income average in the last 5 years of service including overtime and what the employee's average earnings were during the whole period of service. Using the metrics and having a set retirement date, the company pension fund will guarantee the employee a pension income amount based on the pension metric calculations.

In my humble opinion, a defined benefit plan is the best one to have. However, the failure of many pension plans is starting to rise as well as, the reduction of pension payment amounts. Many companies year after year, default on retirement payments to employees due to the pension fund falling short financially or complete failure, thus becoming non-existent. Some of the reasons for shortfalls may be attributed to,

- Senior management redirects pension fund capital to be used in other projects or as venture capital with no payback
- Companies managing and investing the retirement funds make poor investment decisions

- The company does not calculate and forecast the funds requirements correctly. Leaving too little money to accommodate the current or future retirees, thus forced to cut payments

- Unforeseen market and economic forces and instabilities creating massive or even systemic pension fund losses or failure, or

- The company itself fails

The disturbing outcome of these shortfalls is only to abruptly leave their loyal employees with no pension income or to drastically reduce their current or future pension income. On top of it all many retirees have very little savings, which is totally devastating especially in their later years. In truth, these retirees have been loyal to the same company for 20 to 40 years of their prime working life only to end up, broke with no pension and with a broken promise.

As an employee with a defined benefit fund it's up to you to do some research to find out the financial state of your pension fund. In the US, you can do this by requesting the information such as a summary annual report, and look at the return or performance of the fund. You can also look at the minimum funding standards section of the report which states if the fund actually meets such standards. In addition, you can also search the Pension Benefits Guaranty Corporation (PBGC) which is a government agency that insures private pensions in the US. They can be accessed online at www.pbgc.gov

In Canada, there are no guarantees of private pension plans. Only one in the province of Ontario called Pension Benefits Guarantee Fund which guarantees up to $1,000 a month under certain circumstances, whatever that means? Also according to a study by the Dominion Bond Rating Service or DBRS, which states, of 461 plans in Canada, the U.S., Japan and Europe, found the average funding level of pension funds in 2012 had fallen to only 78%. DBRS considers funding levels under 80% to represent a "danger zone." For more information visit the DBRS site at www.dbrs.com.

I have seen defined benefit pension funds fade quickly from the pension world. Many companies are dropping the defined benefit scheme to move to defined contribution. The reason is pensioners are living longer and interest rate returns are very, very low resulting in these pension schemes having inadequate funds available for all of their dedicated hard working employees. This strongly suggests the defined pension will become a thing of the past because of the lack of funds and the company also carries all of the defined benefit plan risks.

Now companies are basically handing over the liability and risk by switching to a defined contribution type plan. This means that it is up to the employee to make decisions based on what shares, mutual funds or other investment instruments will be used for investing for the future of their own pension fund. With a defined contribution plan, employees contribute to their own pension fund and in turn the company contributes by matching the employee's contribution to a maximum yearly amount.

This contribution by the company and the pension vehicle itself is still a good plan, because the employee has more control. However, this also means the employee carries all of the risk and liability. In other words, if poor investment decisions are made by the employee it could result in substantial or catastrophic losses, which may result in the employee's fund having a small amount of money or none at all.

For instance, if an employee decided to buy and invest in tech stock ABC company shares at $110 each then....to find out a few years later that the shares are now only worth $1.50 each. The employee would have full responsibility with the decision to buy the shares in the first place and to cope with the huge loss of over 98% of their pension fund. Keep in mind with this schema, there is no blaming the company, because it is the employee's decision, not the company's.

I use this simple scenario as an example, because most people just make a decision and leave it. They follow ostrich methods of investing by sticking their head in the sand. Employees think and believe that it'll take care of itself. This means the employees don't watch it, and check on it on a regular basis. They at some point in the future will decide to look at their fund to realize they have been slaughtered in the stock market and by then it's too late.

This type of pension scheme is also a disadvantage for many people. The reason is many employees have no real experience with investments and many trust investment representatives at banks and other institutions. They believe these representatives will protect their money and provide instrumental investment advice.

The truth is, investment representatives do not manage a person's money, nor do they have sound knowledge of where to place your retirement money or savings. They in fact only follow company policies and software to set up a portfolio for their client. The software chooses what sectors to invest their client's money according to their client's age and risk threshold.

Many other investment gurus suggest that you have a balanced portfolio. So when you are losing your shirt in one sector, the others, should be increasing in value balancing everything out. I strongly disagree with this because many sectors can free fall simultaneously thus creating a high potential of deep losses. A simple suggestion is that a money market fund is the most stable that doesn't offer much growth but it allows you to retain your money with little loss, if any, regardless of economic turmoil or market downturns.

Each and every time there is a market crash or meltdown, like in 1929, 1971, 1987, 1989, 1990, 2000, 2007, 2008 and 2010 people and companies have lost billions or even trillions. Most of these losses are stock market based investments resulting in wiping out retirement funds belonging to companies, governments, people and even pensioners! Regardless, losses can occur within, government pension funds, defined contribution, defined benefit, and personal pension savings accounts because many are positioned in high risk investments.

So, there is always a very strong possibility of default of defined benefits and defined contribution pension funds because almost all rely on stock market based investing for getting returns. During market meltdowns, like any in history results in, many people are left, time after time, with minimal amounts of cash in pension funds, with no savings, only to start over trying to find a job to make ends meet at retirement age.

For example, I recall during the 1999-2000 downturns where all the high-technology companies were way overvalued, one like a communications company called Nortel. Pensions were buying blocks of Nortel shares at their peak of $124 a share in August 2000. Then to quickly find out that share prices were based on hype, and the shares started to free fall to a value of $0.27. The disintegration of Nortel came to fruition in January 2009 when Nortel did not exist anymore and filed for Chapter 11. So where are all the, pension plan gurus that were managing the plans and buying these Nortel shares and others like it at their peak? Sadly enough, I can only guess that they are still employed managing some other pension plan and getting their commissions and pay.

Another point I want to mention is about government pensions that are comparable to the current defined benefits plans which are also in trouble. I include these because everyone seems to be contributing into something that is mandatory and may not receive anything just when they need it the most. So I have to ask, how does that work?

Well... it doesn't. For instance, in the US according to a Nov. 14th 2014 Forbes article called, "Bad News For State Public Pensions Plans" states that, "In 2013 state pension plans were underfunded by a staggering $4.1 trillion. In 2014 that number has risen to $4.7 trillion. Even though the economy has been improving and there is more talk about state budget surpluses than deficits, states are not addressing this major budgetary issue." The same belief about the Canada pension plan which is the Canadian governments defined benefit plan is that it won't exist when most of the current population is baby boomers that will retire within the next two decades. To learn about how the Canada Pension plan works visit the following site.

http://www.servicecanada.gc.ca/eng/services/pensions/cpp/retirement/

Also an excellent article in the Huffington Post, dated March 30, 2015, entitled, "After 50 Years of the Canada

Pension Plan We've Run Off Course", clearly states the pension situation and how the general public is set up for retirement. This quote from the article tells us a lot about the conditions:

"But the typical 35-year-old today is saving less than half of what their parents did at that age. Three-quarters of those working in the private sector don't have access to an employer-sponsored pension plan. And of those who are within 10 years of retirement, less than one-third have $100,000 or more set aside to sustain themselves. Another third have no retirement savings at all."

If you would like to read the full Huffington Post article, go to the following URL:

http://www.huffingtonpost.ca/ralph-goodale/canada-pension-plan_b_6967640.html

With the majority of Canada's population having no savings while their retirement is imminent, it strongly suggest there will be harsh consequences coming soon for many private or government employees when it comes to their magical pension fund. Additionally, the government plans to increase employee's contribution to the Canada pension plan to make up the shortfalls. To find out more about increases visit the following sites:

http://www.bnn.ca/cpp-reforms-to-provide-little-benefit-for-many-canadian-workers-report-1.525914 http://opinion.financialpost.com/2011/06/09/dont-double-down-on-a-big-cpp-cd-howe-warns/

On another front in the US, an article dated, March 17th 2015 in the LA times, clearly explains the loss of pensions, in regard to the California Public Employees' Retirement System, known as CalPERS. The article states, "As millions of private employees lost their pension benefits in recent years, government workers rested easy, believing that their promised retirements couldn't be touched."

The article continues to state that, with the demand for pension funds growing at astronomical proportions, pensions are becoming a problem for cities across the state of California. Californians owe nearly $200 billion for pensions promised to state and local government workers, according to a nonprofit think tank, California Common Sense. So is there any pension guarantees when the article states:

"San Bernardino could be the first city in California to consider cutting worker pensions in a bankruptcy."

You can find this article at the following URL:

http://www.latimes.com/business/la-fi-pension-controversy-20150317-story.html

To add some more factual data to the pension fund failure a chart from the Pension Benefit Guaranty Corporation lists the top ten pension failures. The totals according to the data for all ten companies pension fund failures are:

- Total amount of claims, $27 billion

- Vested participants, 543,875

- Average Claim per Person, $49,933

So, what happens to all of those employees who are looking forward to that magical day of retirement and are sixty five? Those who have very little built up savings, all relying on their government or company based pensions. Are they supposed to keep working and start saving in their mid-sixties? What happens to those dedicated employees who have worked all their lives and looked forward to a defined benefit pension that has failed or defaulted? Or the retirees of defined contribution pension that have been wiped out by market forces? On top of having market meltdowns and potential catastrophic losses to pension funds there is yet another problem looming with defined benefit pensions that are not indexed.

Indexing

This is another fact about pensions however this topic refers specifically to defined benefit pension plan indexing. Indexing, what does that mean? When the pension plan is indexed it means that the amount the recipient receives will increase based on the rate of inflation or the consumer price index (CPI).

The CPI is derived by the cost of a fixed basket of commodities or goods, such as food, shelter, clothing, and transportation, health care and so on. The CPI or rate of inflation is examined each year by the government or controller of the company pension fund to determine how much the pension fund distributions will increase. In other words the recipient's pension increases along with the increase in cost of living. What does it mean if the pension is not indexed?

Without indexing the plan will pay the recipient a defined amount each month. The same payment amount will continue regardless of the inflation level. Therefore, an increase in inflation, results in goods and services becoming more expensive to the consumer. This directly affects the cost of living for each person but the pension payout is the same amount. This in turn means that the pensioner can buy less and less goods as each year passes.

For example, if Hillary and Bernie who live in the United States were pensioners and retired in the year 2000, then they would be paid in "2000 dollars" not "2016 dollars". Consequently, if they purchased grocery items in 2000 for $100 with inflation those same goods in 2014 would cost them $137.48, an increase of 37.48 %. This means that they have lost 37.48% of their pension income and purchasing power because it was not indexed to account for inflation adjustments. So do your own due diligence and find out if your defined benefit pension is an indexed pension, because if it's not, in the long run, your pension income purchasing power will eventually be depleted.

So keep in mind that the longer you live, the more your purchasing power is reduced. This in fact is one of the main reasons people have very little or no savings or are broke in their later years. As prices rise retirees in turn are forced to subsidize their pension income by using their savings especially in times like today with very low interest rate returns. Inflation can deplete your pension and savings or in other words inflation ends up eating your money.

A last point to mention is about inflation effects and your defined contribution pension or any investment, for that matter. Note that inflation always plays a significant role in your investing, if you want it to or not. Because the truth is, if your defined contribution pension fund, or savings account, rate of return does not meet or exceed the current inflation rate, your money is always losing purchasing power just as a non-indexed pension fund does. The reason for this reduction in purchasing power is the "real interest rate" of the investment, which represents the actual growth rate. Consequently, many people are unaware that a, "real interest rate" exists.

For example, if your defined contribution investment is at a rate of 2% per year and the inflation rate is 1.5% the real interest rate your fund is growing at is calculated as follows:

Real Interest Rate = Current Rate of Return – Inflation Rate

Real Interest Rate = 2% – 1.5%

= 0.5%

Therefore, the real growth rate or real rate of return for your defined contribution pension investment is 0.5%. Remember that inflation is always occurring in the financial system otherwise the system doesn't work.

After discussing all of these pension perspectives, are you ready as an employee to have the rug pulled out from underneath you just before you retire or while you are retired? I would say no. Sure there is a guarantee and that is *YOU*, being in charge of your retirement funds by keeping it safe, sound and continually monitoring the health of your company pension and government based pensions.

Richard Renstone

PART II

Making Your Career Great Again!

and

Your Life Great Again!

Richard Renstone

Page Left Blank

BEST PRACTICES

Employee best practices...what does it mean? Best practices by definition, are the best or most effective way, of performing certain tasks and procedures that are the most efficient, in business or at the workplace. So with this in mind, after over thirty five years of employment experience, I thought I would list some of the things I feel and consider are best practices for employees. I found that the best practices are an effective and efficient way of doing things and many are common sense.

Carrying out best practices will in fact make you a more efficient employee, improve your performance, increase your productivity and have you receive recognition from fellow co-workers and management. This could lead to, pay increases, improving work relationships, working with different groups or teams, a different position of higher stature and so on. Best practices are a positive whichever way you look at them.

There are many common best practices that all employees should execute regardless of their position. This book discusses best practices that will help you secure your job; make you valuable and a better employee. I have included over forty best practices that I feel are valuable and they all start with YOU.

Page Left Blank

GOALS AND OBJECTIVES

Before you can accomplish anything in this world there must be goals and objectives. Goals are like all-encompassing principles that guide your decision making. For example, if your goal is to be a supply chain manager within five years, then the objectives are the specific steps you take to achieve the goal such as, taking supply chain management (SCM) courses at a local college or university to receive a certificate.

The next steps could involve transferring to the supply chain or procurement department within the company where you are employed. Then, proceed to pursue a supply-chain management certification which involves more courses and training. Furthermore, you complete some management courses or obtain a project management professional certification. In this example, your goals and objectives work hand-in-hand giving you direction and steps to achieve your goals.

Having goals and objectives are helpful because employees are usually subject to an annual employee review and assessment. This assessment allows the employer to understand what your objectives and goals are. For example, in the review, your boss will learn about your objectives, what kind of training needs you have, your career goals, what improvements you would like to make, and how you feel about your current job and so on.

TEAM PLAYER

Being an effective and valuable team player at your workplace is one of the most important best practices. This means that you leave your ego at the door, and are one of many that form a team with a common goal. As a team player, you are working collectively and collaboratively with a group force of co-workers to tackle tasks or projects on an ongoing basis. As a team everyone combines their strengths, weaknesses, brilliance and creativity to find solutions, creative ideas, innovations and direction and more.

Like the saying goes, "Many minds are better than one". A team setting is my preferred environment to be a part of, because it actually plays a major role in letting people be themselves, allows people to have fun and enjoy being at work and gives everyone a sense of belonging to a group or team.

BE A HELPER

Be open to helping others and develop a habit of helping. Helping your co-workers and other colleagues is a bonus for everyone. By doing this you are cooperating and helping not only those in need but also contributing to the big picture that boosts your popularity and reputation with all your co-workers.

This best practice sends out a clear message to all colleagues and management that you are supportive, willing to take time to help by contributing your time, knowledge, and expertise. This results in reducing co-worker stress, providing resources to meet deadlines and making colleagues feel supported.

Be aware that there are some individuals who will take advantage of your helpful soul for their own benefit. That's okay because the universe will take care of them accordingly.

SUPPORT YOUR BOSS

Supporting your boss, supervisor, manager, or senior manager and so on, is a best practice. Supporting management is how a true employee hierarchy works. Your boss or manager is responsible for the overall decision making, productivity and efficiency of the department or group. The manager is also responsible for all team members training and performance, as well as, any issues or problems within the department or group.

The team ideally supports the manager and the department. All team members in the department or group have a responsibility and duty to support their boss to the best of their ability, in order to make them shine. So, when the boss shines this is a reflection on the department or group and the whole team in that group or department.

When your department looks good, this migrates up the ladder to the senior manager, director, and all the way up to the VP responsible for that entire division looking good. In others words, an outstanding performance of employees and departments or groups runs uphill and most importantly never goes unnoticed. This enhances your chances of being asked to be a part of other teams or groups in the future.

STORMIN NORMAN

Providing ideas and speaking your thoughts to a group, to your manager, or in a team discussion or brain storming session are an excellent way of showing that you are participating, a team player and that you care. Many people however, are too shy or scared to state any ideas or thoughts because they fear being ridiculed or feeling stupid.

Not to worry since in a true team environment, any idea is a good idea and those who ridicule others, are not team players because they in fact lack self-esteem. When you are blurting out your thoughts and ideas, they may not be the actual idea or ideas the group grabs and runs with, but it is a part of turning a simple discussion into a very lively brain storming session. As you provide your ideas, others will be encouraged to open their mouth as well.

The reason brainstorming works is everyone has an open mind and collaborates with each other. As soon as one person verbalizes an idea or thought, this will trigger ideas and thoughts in others in the group and so on. Besides, there are no egos, all of it is very productive, and lots of fun for everyone. I personally love participating in these kinds of brain storming sessions.

NO HEAD BASHING

Head bashing or being head strong and argumentative is not in your best interest. In fact, head strong type arguing is a sign of weakness and egotism within the individual. This kind of arguing suggests that the individual is trying to change people's opinions, because they believe that their idea, facts, solution or whatever it may be is the only one that is right or the best. Generally this kind of arguing with others is frowned upon, unproductive and only creates anger and tension between co-workers in the workplace.

Sometimes there are exceptions to these types, since arguments, disagreements, heated discussions, being "right all-the-time" and winning is what these types enjoy. They are those you may unfortunately have to work with who are bright but self–centered, egotistical a-holes that in truth are weak individuals. These "know-it-all" types are a one person team and are only liked by very few like-minded ones. They don't care who they hurt or humiliate because they only want to win for themselves.

However, if you offer constructive argument which is healthy disagreement, 99.9% of the time it is well received. In a true team environment, there is no head bashing only the odd disagreement. Most activity is collaboration and participation with everyone in the group all thriving to fix the problem, achieve a goal, and come up with a solution and so on.

Another point about argument is that at times you may have the right solution, idea, facts, comments or evidence to win an argument. Nonetheless, many times it is better not to be the one who wins the argument. I say this because, even though it may not be your intent, it usually ends up in shunning the other person or people, making them feel humiliated or inadequate and so on. In these kinds of situations nobody really wins and it is in your best interest not to focus on winning, but to relay the information openly with no ego, bias or forcefulness.

At times we can also get involved or pulled into situations and discussions with hot heads that usually escalate into an inflammatory argument. In this situation just remove yourself from the discussion by walking away. Or alternatively, you can also let the hot head, "know-it-all" take over and metaphorically let them hang themselves without helping. Besides discussions, arguments, disagreements are a part of having productive meetings. Most importantly everybody is working together because it's not a one person show; it's a team effort.

DO YOUR BEST

Anything that you do at the workplace or even at home, make sure you make the effort to do the best you possibly can. When you have this level of pride in your work at the workplace or at home, this is a direct representation and reflection of you.

In other words, it's about your quality of work, professionalism, knowledge, experience, and your mindset. So, take pride in your work and be proud. One thing I found that works is to try and impress yourself since when you are impressed; it generally means that others will be too, or at least most of your colleagues.

If you always take time and care about performing tasks and producing excellent results, then doing your best will make you shine at the workplace. This in fact elevates your self-confidence and also lets others know, that they can rely on you for doing a great job anytime.

Moreover, this promotes you as, being a team player, hard worker and delivering high quality work. This results in being included in many aspects of the workplace such as other projects, assigned additional tasks and responsibilities and so on.

LEARN, LEARN, LEARN

This best practice is about employees, running the risk of losing their job because of not having the required skill sets or knowledge. The reason this would happen is actually quite simple. The employee feels that training and acquiring knowledge is unnecessary because they have been with the company for a long time, or they have an undergraduate, associate's degree or college diploma and so on. Generally, once people obtain there college or university education that's it. Many feel there is no need to take any more courses or add more skills.

This attitude of disregarding on-going training places these individuals on a precarious and shaky career path. As a result the employee will, lose their ability to seek other employment, become undesirable, replaced, laid-off, demoted, and stuck in the same job with the same pay. This happens because the employee doesn't have the skill sets or knowledge anymore. Also the department may close because of current technological advances.

Training and knowledge is a must in any workplace since you should always be capable of keeping up with technological advances, trends, maintaining your marketability and being a valuable asset not a stagnant one. Besides, if employees don't take courses and upgrade and learn new skills, it can result in employees becoming obsolete, bypassed for promotions or new job opportunities, pay raises and more. On the other hand, those who take courses and continue to add new skills or update their existing skills have no worries of losing their job or being phased out because they are always valuable to the company.

Overall, anyway you look at this, training, upgrading or enhancing new skills is a best practice that you will use and rely on the rest of your life. Technological advances in software, hardware and communications, or techniques, procedures, ideologies never stop changing.

So it's up to you to be at the forefront. This is easily accomplished by changing your mindset to live by a life-long learning philosophy which I have done personally for decades. Remember that:

"Knowledge is power."

ORGANIZATION

Another best practice I found is being organized which refers to items, such as:

- Time

- Your desk

- Emails and information you are keeping or distributing

- Filing cabinet(s)

- Your office or cubicle

- Hosting a live presentation or meeting

- Hosting a meeting or presentation using GoToMeeting, telepresence, Skype, or other applications

Being organized is in your best interest especially when you are dealing with other people, like meetings or presentations of any kind to any number of people.

I emphasize this because I have experienced many in-person and online meetings when all the attendees are present, and everyone is sitting there watching the disorganized host fidget with their computer and/or the equipment trying to get it to work; or the host forgot some printed notes or material that no one else has, or information that was not sent or distributed and so on.

In this circumstance, attendees view the host as being extremely disorganized, unprepared and the meeting inefficient and non-productive. Some people are upset because the host is wasting their precious time. This kind of disorganized situation basically results in very few people attending any future meetings with this host. Keep in mind that when you are the host, some or most of your attendees have very little time.

In other words, the higher up the management position is, the less time they generally have. So wasting their time is unacceptable and very unprofessional. As a best practice, go to the presentation or meeting room location very early, to set up and test all the equipment. Also, make sure that you have all the material you require well-in advance.

Another point to mention is having excellent organizational skills is a must in any workplace. Being highly organized helps you as a team player to be tidy, know where things are, easily find and access certain things you or others may need. Also there is nothing worse than going into someone's office to find chaos, with papers and files all over, where you can't even find anything that you are looking for. This in fact, is a reflection on the person which shows their lack of organization. This sends out a message to colleagues about how the person feels about their work life and even in their personal life.

When things are orderly it means that there is no confusion and clutter only efficiency and a clear, well organized atmosphere to allow for finding things quickly and efficiently, and being able to easily take on new tasks and projects.

Once you are organized and develop a system, stay organized since the organizational skills that you use show you are professional, efficient, productive, and respect people's time because you never waste it.

BE APPROACHABLE

Another best practice is being approachable regardless if you are a manager, director, VP or coworker. When you are approachable it means that you have certain qualities and demeanor. Some of the qualities are being non-judgmental of others regardless of what they discuss with you. When you are non-judgmental this ensures people that you are not going to react in a harsh manner and make them feel humiliated or that you are above or better than they are.

Other qualities involve being complimentary of others work, their performance or achievements no matter how small or insignificant they may be. Be able to laugh at jokes or yourself since as a human being we all make mistakes, forget and make errors. When you are an approachable person you have a pleasant and friendly demeanor. Your qualities also include being empathetic to others by putting yourself in their shoes.

Another aspect is not having any harsh kneejerk reactions to any ones comments or circumstances. As an approachable person you do not humiliate or belittle or make people feel unworthy or stupid. In fact you ensure they are at par with you. These qualities and traits in fact attract people to you who need help, or need a question answered, or your opinion. These are very strong traits to have when it comes to the networking world, especially at the workplace.

The reason is it sends a clear message to your co-workers that your door is open for anyone who needs help. With this colleagues do not feel embarrassed, ashamed or stupid or judged. Your co-workers or subordinates know they can ask for your opinion, advice, help, idea, comments or any input you may have to help them. When a person is approachable it results in being popular among colleagues, viewed as a team player and as someone people can turn to for help or advice regardless of what it may be. Most importantly, people know that you will be willing to take a little time to listen and help out.

HEALTH AND SAFETY

A best practice at any workplace is your health and safety. Health and safety are of the utmost importance to any company and are usually rated as a number one policy at any workplace. Generally, all employees are entitled to a workplace environment where health and safety risks are low and properly controlled.

To ensure employees are safe at work, all health and safety measures are regulated by a government based organization or entity. Some of these organizations and entities are occupational health and safety covered by provincial governments in Canada or in the US, the US department of labor, or in the UK, the Health and Safety Executive.

Employers are responsible for following government based workplace safety regulations to ensure that their employees are in a low risk health and safety environment. Employers are generally responsible for the following:

- Provide employees with a safe method of performing their job

- To make sure employees have awareness of the associated risks to their health and safety

- To ensure employees are aware of how many risks are present and how they are controlled

- Inform employees of the person and entity that is responsible for health and safety at the workplace or jobsite

- To protect all personnel in the workplace

- To hold regular scheduled health and safety checks and inspections

- To have regularly scheduled heathy and safety meetings

- To provide first aid response and treatment as well as emergency protocols

- Supply free health and safety and fire rescue training to employees

- Supply any and all safety equipment required, such as breathing apparatus, gloves, environmental suits, coveralls, masks, boots, eye and ear protection, etc.

- Furnish any other items required for safety and health that is adequate for performing the job

- To have an online health and safety portal accessible by all employees, to document and record employee reports of near misses, accidents, incidents, concerns, injuries, observations and preventative actions and so on

In any health and safety situations at the workplace the employee has the following entitlements and responsibilities:

- The employee can only work in areas where all health and safety risks have been properly analyzed, assessed and controlled

- Employees can stop working if they feel the work area is unsafe or a threat to their own health and safety or others

- To immediately inform their employer of potential or current safety or health risks or concerns that can be rectified to prevent injury or fatality

- To become a company health and safety representative

- The employee is paid regular wages for any health and safety training that is required

- The employee can take breaks from work situations that are arduous, demanding or tiring in nature

- To always have proper facilities at work locations, such as, toilets, wash areas, and potable drinking water

- To have adequate first aid facilities and equipment readily available, such as, eye rinse stations, first aid kits, defibrillator and so on

- To have trained first aid personnel on site

- Employee is aware of the person(s) that are health and safety and first-aid representatives

- The employee should report any near misses, accidents, incidents, concerns, injuries, observations and preventative actions and any other related health and safety items

Health and safety is everyone's responsibility and employees should always be vigilant about their own health and safety, as well as, their co-workers health and safety.

However, in some circumstances there are exceptions. With that in mind I have a few personal experiences to share with you about health and safety.

Friday with a Twist

The first example is in regard to safety when I was working for a field service company that had their shop located in an industrial zone. This was a workplace incident that was out of everyone's control since this was an anomaly which has never occurred in this geographic region.

Days before this event, weather was cyclical, very hot like in the nineties then the temperature would drastically drop into the forties; this again was out of the norm. However, the weather on this particular Friday was sunny like any other day until, clouds suddenly started to roll in very quickly. Of course, no one really thought much about the clouds because it seemed normal. Besides all the weather forecasts stated there would be a thunderstorm in the afternoon.

Many of us assumed it would be a nice thunderstorm heading our way, which for the most part was correct but not like this one. As each hour passed, the clouds were building and getting darker and darker; the temperature started to drop. Meanwhile, we were working in the back shop and then a colleague came in from outside and with excitement said, "Come on outside, you have to see this, I've never seen anything like it".

Immediately all of us went outside to see what it was. To my amazement, the clouds were very dark black, as I have never seen before. As I gazed at this cloud formation it reminded me of the cloud scenes you see when watching biblical movies or *The Mummy* or *Raiders of the Lost Ark*, when the whole sky is black and all the clouds are rotating. After a while, every employee at the company was outside looking south, viewing this bewildering rotating cloud formation. The rotation continued to pick up speed and then, the center of the cloud disc started to droop and then would quickly recede. It would keep repeating this pattern while the sagging clouds were getting longer in length as if they were trying to reach the ground.

This went on for about an hour or so, while everyone was in awe glaring at this phenomenon. Then suddenly the droopy cloud morphed into a long and skinny cloud that touched the ground. Everyone started freaking out, because no one has ever seen anything like it. This skinny threadlike cloud stayed connected to the ground, and began to grow in girth and was slowly traveling towards us.

Now this funnel cloud, headed north directly at us while following a power line path. There were huge flashes every time it ripped a power pole from the power grid. This carried on, while it moved closer and closer to us. Meanwhile the wind started to pick up to an intense speed so we all retreated into the shop building to take cover.

The shop building had a couple of offices in the front and an electronics lab. In the back shop the building had one brick wall separating the wash bay area, and the rest of the building was open concept with corrugated metal walls and roof. There were also eight motorized bay doors to accommodate parking for eight custom built transport trucks that were used for oilfield wireline logging services. However, on this particular Friday afternoon there were no trucks in the shop.

Meanwhile, the wind increased as the skinny funnel cloud became a full blown tornado. The tornado was aligned directly with our shop coming right at us until it reached the highway. At that moment, it shifted to the left of our shop, completely decimating two buildings beside us. Fortunately, the over 200 employees working in those buildings were let go early, for the weekend; otherwise the death toll would have been a lot higher.

I was on the left side of the building. I could hear the sound of this violent beast moaning outside the side door; it was louder than a freight train and sounded like a huge vacuum. I turned the handle of the metal door and slowly pushed the door but it wouldn't open as if it was locked. I had to use firm footing and all my force to push and hold the door open against the high speed winds that were trying to keep it closed. While fighting to keep the side door open I could see and hear the tornado passing; the brute force and ferocious winds were nothing that I have ever seen or experienced in my whole life.

At that point, I could see debris floating in the funnel, thinking it was just small stuff, like garbage, sand, grass, cardboard and paper. I couldn't believe my eyes, I was actually gazing at cars, big garbage bins, and other large items floating and spinning within the funnel. I immediately let go of the door and it was instantly slammed shut by the extreme force of the wind. I turned around; I could see the walls and roof as if they were breathing. At that moment, the brick wall in the wash bay area suddenly collapsed. The atmosphere inside the shop quickly started to become very turbulent and chaotic. All kinds of debris started to fly through the back shop at high speed, because there was a bay door half open.

So, I walked across the shop to close the door, and as I approached it, a quick thought registered, "Hey I could get hurt doing this". Immediately after that, I was knocked out, black, no recollection of what hit me or what happened.

I do remember waking up lying on the floor of the front office area. I was lying there and wanted to close my eyes and go to sleep but a colleague Robert was looking down at me and started to lightly tap my face while saying, "Hey don't go to sleep, stay awake, keep your eyes open…hey, hey, don't go to sleep stay awake, hey, don't sleep keep your eyes open…hey, stay awake". I had no idea what happened to me, I was in shock, I felt like I was a little banged up but in reality I was oblivious to the multiple injuries I had received.

After some time passed I was attended to by a medic that finally made into the area after the wake of destruction. The medic wrapped up my arm and secured my head and neck because of a possible neck injury. So I was lying there with no hand, arm or neck movement so I couldn't even scratch my nose or anything. At one point, everyone temporarily left me there alone, to attend to others in the vicinity.

As I lay there, a stray golden lab retriever showed up, excited, wagging his tail and kept licking my face. All I could do to have the dog stop licking my face was to blow at the lab, try to shoo the dog or tell the dog to get away from me. The lab didn't listen he kept licking my face then I got upset and yelled, "Get the hell away from me because I am going to fuck you when I get out of this!" In truth, the dog was scared just like everyone else and trying to comfort me.

Suddenly some co-workers and a medic appeared and lifted me into the back of a Courier delivery van to be transported to a hospital emergency department, because there were no ambulances available. I remember while driving away from the tornado zone, the van was continually bouncing all over the place driving over the debris that was scattered on the roads.

We finally made it to the hospital and emergency medical staff did a quick diagnosis and admitted me. They immediately injected me with some pain killer. I woke up a while later in the Neuro ward of the hospital. A nurse approached me when I realized that I had sand bags around my neck so I couldn't move my head. I asked her "why can't I move my head from side to side. She replied, "We had to sand bag your neck because; we believe you may have broken or fractured your neck." Then after another injection I passed out again.

I awoke and a while later a nurse came in and uncovering my feet, then she asked, "Can you feel that or anything at all?" I replied, "ffffeel what?" Then she said, while lifting her hand showing me a large needle, "I stuck this right into the bottom of your foot and you didn't feel it". At that point, a new reality hit me straight on; I realized that I couldn't feel my body from the neck down. Immediately I thought I was going to be paralyzed from the neck down to be a quadriplegic.

Here I was 24 years old with the whole world ahead of me now to be stopped and with it all of my dreams gone, wiped away in a matter of a few minutes. I was in physical and mental pain. The grief, hopelessness and anguish, engulfed me. I felt heartbroken, helpless that the person I knew didn't exist anymore. I had become someone else in a matter of minutes. I couldn't live like this. I didn't want to be taken care of by nurses or aids or to be bedridden for the rest of my life. I didn't want to be a burden to anyone.

While the reality of my condition was brought to the forefront to form a new reality, my brother was in the room and overheard the diagnosis. I didn't want to live like this. I said to my brother, "George you have to assist me in taking my own life since I do not want to live as a quadriplegic." I was weak, felt hopeless and didn't have the strength to face up to the reality of living a completely different life from what I knew just a few days ago. I had given up, had no reason to live anymore, and felt suicidal.

Out of nowhere, I heard a man's voice. It was gentle and he said, "I am lying in a bed beside you and through the curtain I overheard your conversation." He continued with his gentle caring voice, and said, "Hey guy relax, and it's not that bad. I've been in this bed for over a year, and I am a quadriplegic. I broke my neck while diving. You don't have to take your life; you ah… get used to it, and… look at life in a different way."

I was so ashamed, humiliated and was humbled by the strength, power and understanding of this man lying beside me. I felt so small, weak with little value for life. I gulped then replied, "Thanks for the support but I don't have the strength that you have to move on, to go forward, because it's not the life I want to live". He gently said, "It's okay, I know how you feel, give it a few days to see what happens and you'll figure out how you feel about things." I humbly replied, "Thanks, you are very kind, I'll do that."

After a week or so of morphine or Demerol, more x-rays and assessments, the medical staff understood my condition. A doctor entered the room and approached me. He said" Good morning how are you feeling? I said "Okay". The doctor continued, "Great, well initially we thought your cervical spine was fractured and we would have to put you in traction to immobilize your neck injury." I replied, "So are you putting me in traction?" The doctor said," No actually instead, after taking some high resolution CT scans we found that there is a hairline neck fracture but not serious enough for traction. You have experienced trauma to your brain stem and spinal cord. This was also recognized because after a week you could move your legs and arms even though you had no feeling." I said, "Doctor it's not as bad as I believed like being a quadriplegic?" He said, "No, it is spinal cord concussion so, after some time you will slowly recover and gain your balance and all functions as the brain stem and spinal cord recovers. We would like to know if you need a home nurse to help you around your house because you will not have functionality for a month or so." With tears rolling down my cheeks I said, "Thanks Doctor, I am happy that I will be normal again."

The doctor responded, "Yes you will recover after the trauma subsides but you are very lucky because if you received the same blow that broke you right shoulder, but in the area of your brain stem injury, it would have severed your brain stem. In that case, you would simply stop breathing. In this state, there would be nothing we could do except to watch you stop breathing or place you on a ventilator to keep you alive while being brain dead." I was absolutely shocked on how close it was to have been killed by this tornado. At that point I believed that it was divine intervention that saved me for a purpose in my life I haven't yet fulfilled.

After a couple of weeks I was released from the hospital. I had to leave the hospital in a wheel chair while wearing a neck brace and arm sling. I had no balance, couldn't walk, and my whole body was sand blasted. My broken shoulder was covered garish purple and yellowish blotches, and I had a gash on the top right side of my head with about 10 stitches. Two weeks later, one of my front teeth was abscessed since the root was broken from a projectile that hit my face during the accident. To add to this, about fifteen years later during an examination my podiatrist asked if I ever broke my right foot. I said no I haven't broken my foot then he asked again and I said no. Then he said that I must have because of the arthritis he could see in my x-rays which are synonymous with a previous fracture. This I immediately guessed was from the tornado accident.

After being out of the hospital and recovering slowly I did eventually gain my balance and all my functions. I returned to work six weeks later even though my broken shoulder had not healed. I had to, because bills were pouring in and I couldn't live on the workers compensation income I was receiving. So when I returned to work, immediately I started to question some colleagues about what happened during the tornado we all survived.

Colleagues detailed that a building the size of an oversized five car garage outside, collapsed and all the debris from the building went through the bay door I was attempting to close. All of the debris hit me, knocked me out black and buried me. The coworkers of mine unburied me and brought me to the front office and placed me on the floor. The whole industrial area was in chaos. All the windows were blown out, people down the street were decapitated, and others were buried folded in half in the wrong direction from head back to toes and so on. Building debris was thrown all over the roads to make them impassable. I was fortunate and even today still feel that it was divine intervention that spared my life and let me gain my health back to normal.

The first thing I remember about the tornado was there was no warning by the weather service or any news. This was a hell of a surprise we all faced and experienced. As far as tornado dynamics go, the statistics stated the tornado touched down for an hour, travelling a distance of 25 miles or 40 kilometers and reached a width of 0.6 miles or one kilometer. The tornado was the first F-4 to touch down in this city or region. It had winds of 236 miles per hour (mph) or 386 kilometers per hour (kph), killed 27 people, injured more than 300, destroyed over 300 homes and created over $615 million (2016 dollars) in property damages.

In this situation, no one at all had any idea of tornado awareness, safety procedures or any related training. All the employees were more caught up in fascination, amazement and fear rather than tornado safety.

If we had awareness of tornado safety we would have chosen an area of protection and immediately opened all the windows and doors. By doing this it allows the high barometric pressure to equalize while the tornado travels through the building. It also prevents the development of a huge pressure differential which usually results in the building being blown apart, such as walls, windows and even roof tops.

Leaving Can Be Painful

This is another safety example I wanted to share while working on an offshore crude oil loading platform off the coast of Venezuela in the Caribbean Sea. We were in the country waiting patiently to perform services since the client asked for us to be onsite. After about two months, the client decided to release our crew because some construction still had to be completed before we could commence work.

All of us were excited to go home and we had just cause since during our stay, anywhere we ate, we would all get food poisoning and even the locals were getting sick. In fact we actually had to resort to visiting a doctor to get meds to help us with the food poisoning from the unsanitary conditions that existed. After the meds straightened us out, we strictly ate at McDonald's or Burger King. The reason, these were the only restaurants we could eat at without getting ourselves sick again.

That evening we started to pack up our equipment and a colleague asked me to help lift a tool box into a storage crate. We lifted the tool box that was full of tools and didn't think anything of it since we have done this so many times before. We continued to pack all of our tools and equipment and were ready. The next morning we were flying out.

The only problem was the next morning when I opened my eyes while I was in bed; I was in so much pain that it would hurt to breathe. If I coughed it would generate excruciating pain. I was lying in bed and realized that I actually injured my back by lifting the loaded tool box the day before. Immediately, I felt so stupid and frustrated. I started to question why we didn't use precautionary measures like, emptying the tool box before lifting into the crate, or using a crane and so on. The answer was obvious, we did this so many times before that it was not on our mind and besides, we were excited and in too much of a hurry to pack our equipment and get home.

So, after returning home and visiting a doctor and a physio therapist I knew what happened and how I injured myself. What happened was, I squished the fluid out of one of my discs or herniated a disc. This created two months of unlimited pain and agony. With this kind of injury I was in continuous pain and it didn't matter what my position was, standing, sitting, lying down or anything. This was one experience I never wanted to encounter ever again.

So the moral of the story was we didn't use proper lifting techniques and procedures for lifting the tool box into the storage crate. If we did use proper procedures, I would have never been injured in the first place. So being lazy, rushing cutting steps, and trying to save time, caused the injury and the prolonged agony.

STTEOAN

This is a health example and you are probably questioning the title of this example. Sure I know that it doesn't make sense but actually this is an acronym for, "**S**hitting **T**hrough **T**he **E**ye **O**f **A** **N**eedle." I am sure you will understand the title of this section by the end of the story.

This all started or happened while I was in *Iran* as a Technical advisor. We were working rotational shifts like six weeks in and six weeks out. The scariest shift was the first one because of all the questions and unknowns. After a while you get accustomed to the laws, religion, culture, airport and work procedures and even pick up some of the local language which is Farsi. Learning some of the language helps you get around and makes it easier to do things like shopping, taking taxis and other things. Everything was working well and I was adjusted to the travel, and being able to get around the airport in Tehran and then to fly down to a city called Ahwaz which was the work location.

After a year passed, we were no longer new at getting around and everything was routine like clockwork. I found that after each six-week shift I would lose an average of about 10 to 12 pounds. For me this became the norm because our diets were not really fulfilled because we were fed one meal a day at supper time by the client's kitchen facilities that provided food to their workers. For over a year we would have meals delivered to our accommodation and at times enjoyed some local cuisine and even some western cuisine.

On this specific day I was approaching the end of the shift with only 10 days left to go before flying out to a European location like Amsterdam, Paris, Frankfurt, or London. In the evening as usual, we received our supper food delivery, and I recall it was a tomato based chicken dish we have had many times before. We were sitting in the kitchen having supper and it tasted good even though I had no idea what was going to happen to me within the next 12 hours. We did the usually routine after supper like sit around play some card games then retire for the evening, go to our own rooms, read a book or magazine.

The next morning everything was normal and we all had coffee and breakfast which was usually goat cheese, jam and Persian multigrain flat bread. After breakfast we got ready and then drove to our work location. We arrived at the workplace and I proceeded to the lab and everything was a normal day until about 10 o'clock that morning. Then I started to shiver and feel cold, and went outside into the direct sunlight. It was 120° F (55°C) and I started to violently and uncontrollably shake. I couldn't understand what was coming over me but I do remember that I asked for a ride back to the accommodation we had. While I was waiting, it was as if my vision started to collapse by shrinking inward just like watching a computer monitor fail. I got into a taxi, was shaking intensely then I finally arrived at the accommodation. I got out of the taxi, paid driver and with little energy went into the house and immediately went straight into bed. I continued to shake and shiver violently and placed a couple of sheets over me and placed my head under the covers and tried to keep warm. I finally fell asleep. Later I woke up and realized that I had broken the fever. However, I didn't realize that I slept for almost three days. Once I awoke, I immediately headed towards the washroom to vomit and defecate.

At that point and beyond, I didn't really know which end to put down first. The vomiting and dry heaving continued and the defecating wasn't normal by any means it was like straight water being expelled from my body as if I had cholera.

I would continue to go back and forth from bed to the toilet every minute or two to vomit and defecate. Whatever this was my body was doing everything it possibly could to get rid of it. During this there was no way to drink water or anything to rehydrate myself; in fact, I couldn't even swallow my own saliva without being sick.

Even with this horrible and life threatening situation I do recall a somewhat odd and funny story that involved Henry one of the lead engineers on the project being in the washroom. I kept calling him and asking him to hurry up to get out of the washroom because of the urgency of having to defecate and vomit. I could hear him acknowledge the urgent request to vacate and he was trying his best. As I waited I could feel that I could not hold on any longer and pressed and held my two butt cheeks together and started bouncing up and down in the kitchen, yelling, "Henry will you fucking hurry up!" and he'd reply " Okay, okay, almost done!"

While this bouncing and yelling act that I was performing was going on, another colleague, Ed was calmly lying on his bed and reading a novel and turned his head to look down the hallway to see me in the kitchen bouncing around squeezing my butt cheeks together. I remember him sort of smiling at me then all at once I yelled, "Henry fuckin forget-it, it's too late!" then I started to run to the front door of the house. When I arrived I immediately kick the screen door open and turned while pulling my pants down at the same time then I let out a huge spray all over the front yard. Relieved I walked back in the house and went into the washroom to clean up. I started to think about what if…someone was coming over to visit and walking up the sidewalk to bang on the door only to have an awful surprise by being sprayed just like I was a skunk.

The vomiting and defecating continued for a couple more days. Finally I was set-up to see a doctor by my Iranian colleague, Mustafa. He came to the house and drove me to an oilfield doctor that was working in a clinic so the doctor could deal with this serious problem. Of course the doctor couldn't speak English so I was really scared and to the best ability I strongly emphasized that I had a severe allergy to sulfa based drugs. In fact, sulfa based drugs are the usual treatment for urinary tract or bowel infection. So if the doctor were to inject me with a sulfa based drug he probably would have killed me due to my physical condition since I lost 35 to 40 pounds in 3 days. So, are you looking for a fast easy way to lose weight?

I wasn't sure if the doctor understood what I was saying about my allergies. The doctor proceeded to give me an injection in both cheeks of my ass and Mustafa explained that the doctor said these injections were to stop me from defecating. After the doctor finished he handed me a couple prescriptions written in Farsi that I couldn't read. Mustafa drove me back to the house to gather my things so I could pack for the flight. This was all happening in the morning just before my flight to Tehran so I could start my days off.

Exhausted, I proceeded to the airport and caught the flight to Tehran. I settled in the hotel we usually stayed in and all my clothing hung off me as if I was a coat hanger. I asked the front desk agent if there was a pharmacy close by the hotel. The agent said it was across the street. I went up to my room and dropped my suitcases and went downstairs. I walked across the street to the pharmacy and approached the main counter. I handed the pharmacist the prescriptions. I waited for about 5 minutes then the pharmacist returned. He had one box of pills and 3 large saline-glucose solution IV bags complete with the tube and the needle. I was shocked! I couldn't believe my eyes looking at these IV bags with the tubing and needle at the end. This was stuff like the one you see in an actual hospital. So I picked up the IV bags and pills and went back to my room. I thought to myself, what am I supposed to do with these IV bags, I don't know how to inject myself isn't this supposed to be done in a hospital by medical professionals?

I looked at the pills and couldn't distinguish nor decipher if they were sulfa based pills so I discarded them because I didn't want to take a chance. I couldn't use the IV bags either because I had no medical training. Regardless of the pills and IV bags I knew my system was becoming more stable, because now I could actually keep saliva down and water. So I started to drink warm water mixed with table salt and sugar which I was able to keep down. I continued drinking the salt, sugar and water solution for the next couple of days in an attempt to rehydrate myself. On the fourth day in Tehran I started to order soup to the room and was able to hold down the broth. I was completely exhausted and almost lost my life. A few days before my departure I continued eating broth, drinking tea with sugar and warm water with salt and sugar.

I flew from Tehran to Amsterdam then took connector to Milan, Italy to meet my father. When he saw me he was in tears looking at my loose clothing hanging on my body, and said that I looked like a scarecrow. After a hug we went to a restaurant to dine on some fine Italian cuisine.

The information that I gained from this experience besides almost losing my life or having permanent organ damage, was we all ate the same meal. This meant that the part of the meal I had eaten was a bad piece of chicken with E.coli or some other bacteria deposit like feces. I say this because the culture of that country and region dictates that people do not use toilet paper but instead use their left hand and water to do their duty. This would strongly suggest that I could have eaten someone's feces too because of how violently ill I became.

When reflecting on these, regardless of the situations or the circumstances, always be aware of your health especially when working abroad. Remember that your health and safety are most important in any circumstance. As far as safety, never cut corners, be rushed or save time by bypassing procedures or trying unproven alternative methods. The reason is, it immediately increases the health and safety risk of those individuals involved which could result in serious injury or even death. Always take your time and follow all precautions and procedures when performing any tasks at the workplace. Your health and safety is more important than anything in your life is, because without it…

You Have Nothing!

GO THE EXTRA MILE

Making excuses, or listing all the reasons why you can't do something is a negative mindset and this is projected to co-workers. On the other hand, going the extra mile indicates that you are serious about your job, your performance and that you will do whatever it takes to get the job done. Besides when you go the extra mile you are a doer and know the reason why you can do it, not why you can't. Be a person of action!

Going the extra mile can be doing extra work, staying after work or working a weekend because of some deadline that's due on Monday or you are covering one of your colleagues because they are having personal issues or are sick; Maybe a group needs more help in order to accomplish a goal, and because you are a person of action you join right in to go the extra mile with that group.

This reminds me of working for a pipeline service company in the energy industry. This was an ISO 9001 certified company. It was a prerequisite for almost all of their clients because without it clients would not do business. So it was imperative to have the ISO certification and in the company's best interest to never lose the certification status.

I don't recall ever hearing about ISO, nor did I know anything about the ISO system until I started working for this company. However, prior to this, I did use similar type systems. The ISO system is a quality management system and recognized internationally. It is used by companies to ensure they have a structured document system, including policies, procedures, and work instructions. This system standardizes all documents and procedures, which help companies, guarantee consistency and repeatability with their company processes, product quality or services.

I found this system to be quite interesting and took it upon myself to learn and understand it inside and out. Under my own initiative I became the most experienced ISO 9001 person in the company besides the Operations Manager. I wasn't waiting around to be told to participate or to perform tasks. I was interested and motivated, so I spent hours of personal time to understand the system structure to a point where I was in charge of analyzing and ensuring the system was updated, correct, had no gaps and ready for ISO audits. On top of it all, I also produced over 90 percent of the ISO documentation that was required for the system and those same documents were used for training field staff. By taking on this work and going the extra mile paid off. I became an ISO 9001 specialist for the company and shortly after; I received a raise, and was promoted to Training Coordinator.

Another example, was when I started at my first real career industry job as an electronics technologist. I was hired by an oilfield service company and started working in the oil industry. I was introduced to a whole new world of scientific technology. I was very determined to go the extra mile to learn as much as I could and as fast as I could. I worked long hours and studied hard to learn about the scientific instruments and equipment I was hired to repair and maintain. This effort was all so I could achieve sound knowledge and move from a trainee technologist position to a junior technologist level position. I achieved the junior level within 7 months while the average timeframe was 12 to 18 months. This resulted in being fruitful. I received a salary increase and it opened up the door to working overtime.

Furthermore, as a junior, I was taking on as many tasks as possible to demonstration my skills and knowledge to instill confidence in upper management. This allowed me to enter the bidding process for a Middle East technical advisor position with only 2 ½ years of experience. Usually the bidding process consisted of senior employees which have a minimum of 7 to 10 years of experience. In the end, I won the bidding for the international position and it paid off. The salary was $12,000 a month net pay which is equivalent to $23,288 in 2016 dollars plus an additional $25,000 per year in flights or adjusted for 2016 dollars it would be equivalent to $48,500. So the remuneration for the international position changed my financial world, employment status and lifestyle.

If you are a person who doesn't go the extra mile or have any interest in going the extra mile, this suggests that you may be an employee who does a minimal amount at work, and then go home. With this kind of attitude, there is no reason to ask why you don't get pay raises, and opportunities because you are stuck in the same position, with the same salary with no opportunities.

Going the extra mile allows the employee to exhibit a greater strength of character, mental growth, promotes a positive attitude, and to experience stronger convictions of courage and self-reliance. When you go the extra mile it contrasts with many other co-workers who do not.

Going the extra mile also builds trust with co-workers, reassures them that you are reliable and willing to put in extra time and effort to achieve what is at hand. Most importantly, it is almost like building up a quasi-bank account of favors that you can use when the time comes. However, be aware that some co-workers will try to prevent you from getting there because of their own weaknesses and envy. Some may even resort to name calling.

NETWORKING

So what is networking? Networking is the art of meeting people or "putting yourself out there". In other words, when you meet people, you attain contact information to build your work, business and/or personal contacts list. Networking is a big advantage any way you slice it because it opens up a multitude of avenues for everyone. Networking is both external and internal to your workplace.

Internal company networking involves going to meetings whether they are for your department or all company employees. For instance, networking happens at a town hall, a company function like a Christmas party, training classes, a team building outing or other company functions. Having an internal network can lead to department transfers, new opportunities, job changes, pay raises and in some cases climbing the corporate ladder.

When it comes to external networking it usually happens at networking events such as, Toastmasters, Chambers of Commerce functions, conferences, training classes, lounges, non-profit charities, industry shows, employment conferences, and social media.

The whole network process starts by forming your own network which includes co-workers, friends, family, ex-coworkers, professional references, new acquaintances, group and affiliation members, and so on. It also includes being introduced to new contacts through your current job. Having a network provides you with many resources, benefits and hidden job opportunities.

At one point the hidden job market was a telephone book. By calling specific companies I found many jobs before they even started a search or were even considering a new position or hiring someone. I would get a tip, be provided with a contact name, show up at the company with a resume and I at times would be interviewed immediately and be hired on the spot.

Now the landscape has changed. The hidden job markets are through the internet such as, *Indeed, Workopolis, CareerBuilder, Jobsite, Monster, Glassdoor, SimplyHired* and many others. There are also other avenues like work sites such as, *LinkedIn*. LinkedIn is used by over 450 million[1] career professionals, companies, employers and employees in over 200 countries around the world. LinkedIn is the largest site of its kind but there are other social sites such as, Facebook (1.7 billion[1]), Twitter (317 million)[1], Pinterest (110 million[1]), and Instagram (500 million [1]), which are both personal and professional networking sites. In fact all of these sites combined have over 2.6 billion users. This is very impressive especially when there are only a total of 3.4 billion[2] internet users worldwide. Of course, all of these stats I listed will continuously change.

Online network sites provide you with access to a real time hidden job market which allows you to literally have a job opportunity gold mine at your fingertips. By being able to get a network job tip you can be at the right place at the right time before anyone else just like an insider. This may result in being hired immediately by the company before they start advertising.

In this situation, the company is saving time, money and resources because there is no need for an advertising campaign, hiring an employment or placement agency,

---

[1] 2016 statistics from https://www.statista.com/

[2] 2017 statistics from http://www.internetlivestats.com/internet-users/

conducting many interviews, having multiple credit and background checks, as well as, making decisions. Moreover, it immediately solves the company's hiring problem, by filling the resource gap and removes any headaches of searching for the right candidate.

Also this allows active and motivated people to get out there to connect, building long-term relationships with their network associates. Building long-term relationships means that you have to spend time with your network people and keep in touch on a regular basis, whether it's through email, texting, telephone, going for a bite or a quick coffee so you both can get the "skinny" on things.

Another fact about your network is it gives you the opportunity to promote yourself and to help your network members. The reason being networking is like a two way street by giving and receiving. When you help others it makes you feeling good about yourself and to build your self-esteem and self-worth. Remember when helping others, favors are always returned.

Networking also gives you a pool of resources from all different areas of industry, positions, careers, knowledge and decades of experience. This is a very important aspect of networking because it provides access to a large knowledge base which means that you can ask questions about certain topics, to get feedback, insight, best practices, and gain new wisdom, all from experienced people. It also allows you to acquire a different perspective, change your ideologies or to give you new ideas to put into motion. This benefit of networking is very powerful only if you are capable of doing it and know when to employ it.

Networking is free but a successful network takes a lot of time and effort to grow and maintain. Networking is a continuous process because of the diversity of members and dynamic nature of it. This means people within your network are coming and going because of changing positions and contact details, relocating to a new city, state or province. They also have a large array of individual qualities and traits such as, personality, age, gender, career status, experience and education level, religious beliefs, morality, attitudes, expertise, and specializations. Overall it is a must to spend time on maintaining your network and relationships.

With that in mind, a person wanting to be a networker must have certain personality traits themselves in order to be effective and successful at networking. For instance, if you are an introvert being quiet, shy and unassertive, the chances of being an effective networker are quite low. On the other hand, your networking expertise may not be face to face but online instead which is quite effective and successful. Regardless, don't give up because traits you may lack can be learned through training classes and courses, or by having a personal coach and so on.

Some of the main qualities required for being an effective networker are being outgoing, assertive, diplomatic, approachable, friendly, amicable, as well as, having a positive mindset but most importantly being a skillful listener. Again, if you are not a keen listener this is another skill that can be learned through training or coaching.

These traits and skills are applied in every networking situation you encounter because most times you are engaged with many people and listening to what others are saying. You also listen for what the topics of conversations are so you can integrate into the conversations and say things that have substance when it's your turn to speak up.

Keep in mind that networking is not easy nor is it ego driven. It is about other people and promoting yourself, not a one-upmanship game. Since competitive types of behaviors usually insult or offend people and the outcome usually results in being exactly opposite of what you would like to achieve.

When you are actively networking you have to use a trial and error method of finding out what works and what doesn't. Remember that it is in your best interest to be yourself and to be honest, regardless of the people stature. It doesn't matter what position or title is held by your new acquaintances like President, Senior VP, CEO, and CFO and so on, because it's all about people and helping one another. Besides the higher up the corporate ladder people are the more approachable and down to earth. So keep in mind that everyone is equal, and on the same playing field.

Be aware that networking is not about pressure and being forced to do it. Rather it should be viewed as having fun and conversing with others because everyone is there for the same reason. It is to get to know one another, to help each other, find opportunities and distribute knowledge. When you are being yourself, you are being natural in how you express your points of view and show your shining personality. With this approach you are most effective at communicating and establishing a positive first impression.

Networking is where first impressions are made. While speaking to new people, be sure to have business cards with social media links, email and other contact information. These items are fundamental for face to face meetings and are a necessity for staying in touch with your new found contacts.

One of the most important things to keep in mind when you are talking to someone is remembering their face and name. The reason is a person's name is the most important word in the whole world to that person. So, when you forget someone's name, it may offend the person and could even lead to losing the contact. On the other hand, unless you are a forgetful clown like me and can admit it. When it comes to forgetting names when I see a person again I openly can admit to the person that I am a moron when it comes to remembering people's names, songs, actors, movies, and so on. On top of it all I am not embarrassed because I know who I am and what my faults are.

My last point is when having a conversation with someone, if you say things like you will call them, do coffee, go for a drink, get together, send them an article or link of some kind, do it! If you don't, it will impact your reputation and they will have no confidence in you and your word.

EMAIL AND NETWORK STUFF

Email and networking responsibilities is not about your professional network, as we discussed in the last section but this is about your employer's internal computer Ethernet or network. So if you hold a position to use a computer at your workplace, then the IT department will assign you with a computer (asset), login ID and password to access the company network.

The IT department is also there to protect the company network. They are responsible for setting up servers, policies, firewalls, access controls, and security protocols, and hardware. These are all used to fight cyber-attacks, viruses, Trojans, phishing, hoaxes, spyware, spam, scams, hacking, malware and other threats. The IT department plays a major front-end role in network security but another part of security is up to you the employee.

This means that it is the employee's responsibility to follow company IT security policies and guidelines to ensure network security. This means that the IT department will put in some controls for blocking employees from accessing certain websites due to security risks, strip email attachments, or quarantine certain emails, and so on. So it's up to the employee to keep the network safe and here are some basic best practices to follow for your security and personal security.

After onboarding, an employee is usually assigned a user name and a simple password for network login and access. On initial login the employee is forced to change their password. The IT department sets up password protocol requirements that must be followed, such as, length of the password, adding capital letters and using symbols and so on. The employee must periodically change their password in accordance to IT requirements like once a month to maintain password security.

Login information is very important because it is specific data about each employee. Never give out your login information, passwords or any such information to any one for any reason. This also would include personal or any other information regardless even if it's a request via email or texting, or a phone call. In fact, even your IT department doesn't know what your password is.

Email attachments are another aspect of email to watch. Many of us receive email with attachments which are pictures, video, or other media types. Many of the attachments are those which are java, flash based or have macros and are a main culprit for spreading virus or malware. Usually your IT department will have a block on these attachments to prevent virus and malware, etc. Also never open any attachment that comes from an unknown email address, regardless because if you don't recognize it don't open it instead delete it immediately. Also ensure that your "download attachment automatically" on your email settings is turned off. If you receive some peculiar or unknown email, contact the IT department immediately to inform them.

Email scams are a dime a dozen these days, like job site related emails. If you are registered on job sites or are looking for work through online job sites like Indeed, Monster, CareerBuilder, etc., there are also many scam emails that use their information and logos. There is also random email spam which asks for your resume or CV and personal information just as if you are applying for a job which is not authentic. I have received numerous bogus emails from scammers representing companies like Conoco Phillips, Facebook, LinkedIn, Marshalls, Target, Imperial Oil, or Shell Oil and other large European and Middle East oil companies.

The reality is that companies don't send random emails asking for your resume or CV or any personal information. However, if you have signed up with a specific company to receive job notifications, then you will receive notices because you registered with that company. Additionally, companies never contact you directly by telephone but only if you have applied for a job and they are interested in hiring you and arrange an interview. Again do not disclose information to anyone unless you know the agency rep or the company. Do your own due diligence.

If you work on a computer at the workplace here are a few important security points to follow about your computer.

1. Always lock your screen if you are walking away from your computer or leaving your office to get a coffee, drink, take a bathroom break or going for lunch
2. At the end of your work day, always close all software programs, even if you are going to be using them the following morning. This prevents your open files from being corrupted by a possible power outage or an abrupt system shutdown.
3. Be sure to physically power down your computer or laptop or tablet and any external monitor(s) and printers. These actions save power and increase security because your computer is off the grid.
4. Minimize any personal use of your work computer and avoid signing up at sites with your work email address. This will reduce spam.

The more awareness, training and understanding you have about safe email and internet best practices will make you a zero security risk at work.

What many people don't understand is the IT department at your workplace is continuously fighting threats, cyber-attacks, spam, scam and hackers on an hourly basis. Nonetheless, I feel that regardless of what company or what security is being used; all of us are in some sense sitting ducks especially if professional hackers choose to concentrate on your company's network. Besides, these professionals can hack into the most sophisticated systems around the world just ask the Clinton's, Pentagon, WikiLeaks, Yahoo, Home Depot, and many, many others.

DODGY CHARACTERS

Another office security topic deals with people that are always coming and going throughout the workplace such as electricians, plumbers, construction workers and other paid contractors performing services at your workplace. The point I am making is very important because not all of these workers are supposed to be at your workplace. Scammers can pose as workers or contractors that aren't workers at all but instead are thieves. Also these so called construction contractors and other people working at your workplace may be doing legitimate work, but occasionally are also thieves.

If you see people with suspicious or erratic behavior around your workplace, don't hesitate to contact your manager or building security. Since I have worked at a multitude of companies where theft occurs in the work place and it can be by employees like those that I speak about in the Alibaba section, or could be 3rd party companies or just wandering thieves.

For instance, at one employer I recall things suddenly started to disappear, items like jackets, purses, wallets and some computer equipment. It was a data company which required the latest technology and most powerful computers on the market in order to deal with massive data volumes and analysis. The computer related theft was not detected until one morning, when the data analysts started their computers to find that they did not boot up into a windows environment instead sat idly with a black screen and blinking curser waiting for further instruction.

The peculiar thing about the computer related thefts were that none of these computers were stolen but only the CPU processor chip inside the machines. So with that in mind, it meant that the person who was stealing was internal to the company and had full knowledge of procedures to safely extract the CPU processor chips. This strongly suggested that the thief would have extensive computer hardware knowledge, a specialized chip extractor, and electrostatic sensitive device training.

I say it's an internal theft because the computer-processor chip theft would mean that the perpetrator would be undoing all the screws on the machine, taking the covers off, and then extracting the chips on each of the machines which would take a lot of time. I even to this day feel that there were a couple of possibilities related to the variety of thefts that took place at this company.

First of all, the wallets, jackets, purses and other things could have been a diversion or there was a separate theft from a third party contractor or some wanderer just randomly accessing the office area. For instance, the purses, wallets and other items were usually in a coat pocket or purse; or in a toolbox giving the thief, easy access to the items and could steal them within seconds. The perpetrator would then walk straight out of the office area undetected. These items I felt were stolen within seconds that in fact is typical for thieves because the system is to grab items and vacate in the least amount of time possible without being caught.

With all of the thefts that happened, the only way the company could deal with this was to first, hold a meeting with all the employees to inform them about the situation and what the solution was. Then the company had to ratchet up security by installing keycard door locks on main doors and video cameras, as well as, a security system. So this theft resulted in having all employees live with the fact of reduced privacy since there were cameras all over the workplace and to swipe their card at every main door.

Another thing to watch out for is how people gain entry to the office area. For instance, you may see a person standing at a card locked door waiting for someone to let them in. This situation happens quite a bit and it is very difficult to memorize all people who may work in the building. However, thieves stand at card locked doors waiting for someone to let them in which is called "piggybacking". This is where the person or thief is allowed entry by the person who opens the security door with their card. The person piggybacking may be well dressed or appear as a construction worker or trades person. They are usually very polite but only interested in gaining access into the work place to steal. When in this situation, do not allow the person in the door and instruct them that they do not look familiar to you and that you are sorry but they should contact building security or a co-worker to gain access. This kind of action is usually a standard security protocol that everyone is instructed to use.

So if you see any questionable characters wondering around your workplace or some suspicious behavior make sure you contact security, and question them directly and tell your manager immediately. Do not let them in!

YOUR STUFF

Every employee carries some kind of valuable with them at the workplace, which can be their wallet, credit cards, watch, jewelry, check book, cell phone or other items. I am not trying to make you paranoid but as a best practice, it is better to leave expensive jewelry, watches, or other such items at home and not bring them to work.

If you are bringing things of value to work, like earrings, jewelry, watches and other items, never remove them and always wear them. Another point is to keep your wallet or purse close at all times while at the workplace. Never leave any items unattended or out of reach.

If you must leave your items for a moment like for a bathroom break or lunch, always have them in a desk drawer or locker and locked it up. If your desk doesn't have a locking drawer, get one installed by your employer. Remember to always lock-up your valuables whenever you leave your office, even if it's only going next door to ask a colleague a question.

CAPTAIN'S LOG

When we are at work, there are always so many details and other things that we should remember, that continue to accumulate throughout our work day. Many of us just use and rely on our memory to keep track. Regardless of our age, it's merely impossible to remember all of the tasks, events, meetings, schedules, incidents and details about things that happen during our work day.

This best practice is to always keep a detailed log of what your tasks were and other details about what happened, what you did, completed, achieved, or what is pending, what is required, who you were in a meeting with, who attended, what was discussed and so on.

Most importantly, continue to log everything you do each day. This should be detailed enough so if you must refer back to it, you will understand what was going on. Don't worry about the time it takes to log your day because it's all a part of doing your job. Besides, your colleagues, supervisor or manager will be pleased, impressed and others may follow your lead.

Another point to add is, before going home; write down all of your tasks, meetings, presentations or anything else you have to do for the next day. This works very well since it provides you with a fresh list of items that have to be completed. After you arrive at work the following morning, you can have a coffee or tea and sit down and review the list; while preparing a plan before starting your workday.

This in fact helps you hit the ground running every morning without forgetting anything because you know what you have to do or achieve that day. Continue to list all items in your day timer for the next day before you leave. This means you will never forget, or be blank about what was supposed to happen or whom you were going to talk to or what meeting you were scheduled to attend and so on.

Keeping track is easiest on your computer, tablet or cell phone using a calendar like Microsoft Outlook, or other software programs or apps. You can also use a paper notebook and jot down all these items. I on the other hand, use the old school hardcopy kind, a Brownline

C530F big ass day timer that has a hard cover that costs around 40 bucks. It provides a full page (13.4"x 8") for each day of the year. This gives me plenty of room to make notes, lists and anything else that comes up. I also store the Brownline day timer each and every year which results in having a complete set of history for reference. Overall, your log is also a part of being organized.

ANSWERS

This best practice is to have an open mind. This is to understand there is always a multitude of answers and solutions to any kind of situation or problem at the workplace. You want to be free thinking, able to hear what others opinions are, what they think and how they view certain situations or circumstances. This is a part of being collaborative, a team player and working in a team environment.

However, there is another side to this. There are others who are not free thinking and have limited views. These individuals most times are detrimental to group discussions. They view the world as either this or that, on or off, or all or nothing. In fact, they only have two possible conditions or states to problems or situations they encounter. People who have a two choice world look at the world as being all black or all white with no in-between.

These individuals are generally not team players or collaborative and usually argumentative which doesn't work. These individuals have a limited and narrow outlook and are considered to be closed minded. In reality, the world is not all comprised of two possible states because there is a multitude of conditions, states, solutions, answers, ideas to solve any circumstance or situation we encounter.

Most importantly, know that it's not black or white but always includes multiple shades of grays and colors that make up the answers either in the workplace or in life for that matter. So, by having an open mind it may set you up as a key employee, participating in high level discussions for the department, group or company.

APPEARANCE AND HYGIENE

This best practice deals with an employee's appearance and hygiene. To some of you, this may sound absolutely ridiculous but… it really isn't because your appearance and hygiene says a lot about you as a person and professional.

The most basic point about hygiene is the way you smell. I am not talking about perfumes, deodorant or aftershaves but how your body and breath smells. First if you don't brush your teeth regularly or have cavities or gingivitis then your breath will be disturbing to many, especially for those unlucky colleagues that work very closely with you.

If you are a smoker and drink coffee that is another very unpleasant smell that turns people off completely. Believe it or not your breath alone can make co-workers avoid you; avoid speaking to you or to distance themselves when speaking with you. Do you really want people to avoid you and probably talk about you with others because of your bad breath? The solution is very simple; all it takes is brushing your teeth regularly and some mints or mouthwash or medicated mouthwash. You can always have your dentist assess to see if dental problems are causing it.

Taking showers or bathing is another basic part of hygiene. If people don't shower or bathe on a regularly basis, they start to smell. You may be sitting in disbelief, but I have experienced lack of showering in many of the companies I have worked for, and it doesn't matter what gender, or what kind of workers from skilled trade's people to office staff, like admins, executives and others.

Not taking a shower or bath once a day or every other day, promotes unpleasant body odors or BO such as, sweat, greasy hair, dandruff, smelly feet and bottoms, which all permeates your clothing. This can actually disrupt a whole room of people or group because of the smell being so pungent. Ewww…People remove themselves from the vicinity, some will actually make sounds, comments and others will confront the person about the way they smell. Do you really want to be known by the nickname, "Stinky"? Or have people continually avoid you? Do you want to be in an awkward position when your manager or boss has to speak to you about your basic hygiene? I think not. There are other effects that the lack of bathing has on our body.

It promotes various bacteria, fungi, yeasts and parasites to grow and multiply on your skin. These are harmless on your skin but if they were to enter the blood stream they can be fatal. Scabies can leave you with itchy hands and feet and head lice can spread to others and to not so nice parts of your body! As for BO, it's not really our sweat that smells it's the bacteria that start eating our sweat then produce waste which smells. Not washing allows bacteria to increase on our skin thus creating conditions that may cause skin infections to flourish.

Also, if a person already has an existing skin condition like acne and doesn't wash, it may intensify the condition. Another skin condition that may appear on the skin are patches of thick, brown plaques which consist of sweat, bacteria and dead skin cells that form on localized areas of your skin. So all it takes is showering or bathing regularly, using scent free antiperspirant, and clean clothing but most importantly, the desire to be clean and to feel good about you.

Another part of hygiene is about your clothing, is it clean and pressed, new, old, and full of dog or cat hair, dirty, stained or stink? Do your nylons have a run? Do you have stains on your tie or collar and when was the last time your ties were dry cleaned? Are your shoes dirty, stained, worn, clean, and polished? Is your clothing or outfit provocative, wrinkled, revealing, too tight, too small, or what kind of message does your clothes send out? Does your outfit or clothing look professional? Is it appropriate for the job, or meeting? One point to make here is, don't wear or recycle the same clothes more than twice because chances are very high that it will be smelly.

There are other things like your hair. Is your hair, clean, greasy, brushed, messy, have dandruff, groomed, smelly, styled, cut, over grown, multi-colored like a rainbow? Does it look like you just got out of bed? Is everyone calling you "Bedhead" or "Einstein" because of your morning hair?

If you wear makeup, is it applied evenly, precisely, wrong shade or tone, too bright, too dark, doesn't match, or too much of it? The way it's applied, does it make you look happy, sad, unhealthy, angry, creepy, or healthy? Do you really need it? Are you trying to hide your true looks?

Are you clean shaven, have an ungroomed beard, overgrown eye brow hairs, have hair growing out of your ears, or nose? Do you have snot hanging out of one of your nostrils? Ewww!

Do you have piercings all over your face, nose, and mouth, on your tongue or cheeks? If it's cultural who cares but if it's not well…Do you have tattoos all over neck, arms, face and your body? Are they tasteful, or making you look like you are crying out for attention? Can your tattoos be hidden or covered?

One last thing to mention is to wash your hands frequently, and keep your hands away from your mouth, nose, and eyes to avoid viruses or infections. When there are no facilities present like being in a field location, use waterless hand sanitizers. Along with cleaning your hands make it a habit to wipe down your telephones, desk top, mouse, computer keyboard, stapler and other items that are always being touched. This will help you to avoid getting sick.

All of these things I have listed matter regardless of your gender, profession, employer or position, whether you are a teacher, welder, doctor, engineering, flight attendant, laborer, technician, executive, manager, supervisor or factory worker.

These things may sound basic but in fact upkeep of your appearance and hygiene are the most important practices for anyone. Your appearance and hygiene is like a presentation to others and is a reflection of, who you are as a person, and how you feel about yourself. Have you ever heard the saying, "A picture is worth a thousand words"?

The truth is, these basics can and will make a world of difference for you and your fellow co-workers for opening up opportunities. You will find that you are radiating confidence; people are more courteous, complimentary, interested in speaking with you, working with you and may even want to get to know you on a personal level. All of these things are positive anyway you look at it.

Keep in mind that people in general, usually make snap judgements about a person's appearance within the first fifteen to thirty seconds of seeing them. These quick observations and occasional stereotyping, can reveal things about you such as, your level of confidence, professionalism, success, and flexibility, or if you are creepy, wealthy, easy, intelligent, reliable, truthful, mentally stable, organized and so on.

So, when getting ready for work, you put on your work clothes, and do your hair, etc., remember that your appearance sends a message to your colleagues and management. It will tell people a lot even if their interpretation about you is incorrect. These assumptions can in many cases be the difference between getting the promotion, attaining a new job or not, or people not taking you seriously or giving very little weight to your opinions, ideas or thoughts. In fact, your appearance can keep you doing menial jobs the rest of your life even though you are qualified for something else. Don't get me wrong here every job has value and dignity.

However, when keeping up your hygiene and appearance, it may lead you to be a person of interest and further your career like the saying goes, "Dress for success". This is true in that dressing well and keeping excellent hygiene will make you feel confident and attractive. It will make feel good about you, which leads to improving our self-image, self-confidence, and general outlook on life.

Remember that appearance and hygiene are the basics of being a human being so take them seriously. Because all of these things we have discussed relay a message to the outside world. So ask yourself this: Am I sending a true reflection of who I really am? Is your low level of hygiene, or purple hair or tattoos, body piercing more important than getting a promotion, a high paid job, being recognized as a serious professional in your particular field of expertise, or your training and background? It's all up to you to change.

MAKES SCENTS TO ME

Sure... it makes scents to me. Your probably asking what makes sense? Well, I am referring to the increase of, "Scent-Free" policies at many companies. This in fact is becoming the norm in most workplaces. Why have scent-free workplaces? The answer is quite simple.

Employees and colleagues especially in office environments have the air filled with an abundance of smells from fragrances and perfumes, soaps and lotions, aftershaves and deodorants, hairsprays and even cleaners and air fresheners. As a result, our noses are bombarded with a plethora of scents which in fact have different chemical ingredients that affect some people's health.

Some health problems caused by these scents are headaches, dizziness, nausea, upper respiratory symptoms, and shortness of breath or even skin irritation. Moreover, the severity of these symptoms will vary from mild to debilitating. Also, certain scents may trigger "attacks" for individuals that have certain allergies and Asthma.

The outcome of having various scents throughout the workplace is they may mildly affect certain employees by causing them to have a stuffy nose or a headache. On the other hand, it could result in an adverse effect on the employee by having them incapacitated and requiring medical assistance. The best practice is to refrain from wearing any scented perfumes, fragrances, deodorants, aftershaves, hairsprays, etc., at the workplace; instead try using products that are fragrance-free, to maintain neutrality. This is shows coworkers courtesy, compassion and understanding, and following company policies.

I'LL BE IN THE KITCHEN

Another point to add overlaps with the office scent free environment policy of many companies. The point I am making involves food preparation and dining by employees within the workplace. Sure now you may feel you can't eat or prepare any food at work? No you can eat but what you make to eat does matter. This is quite simple since; many of us think that everyone feels like we do, about many things, especially food.

Sorry but that's not the case especially when it comes to cultural cuisine. Yes, you may feel that everyone loves that dish you are preparing in the workplace kitchen and you may even receive some positive comments on the smell of the dish and how yummy it looks.

However, not all people feel that way and depending on the dish it could be unpleasant to some, and even create allergic reactions. Most importantly, it can also make the whole office smell like the dish and even colleagues clothing. So as soon as the dish's aroma engulfs the office, this means that by making this meal, you are invading everyone's airspace which is not acceptable. This is why most times companies have designated dining areas.

If there isn't a dining area go outside, eat out or keep your meals simple, be courteous and follow office etiquette. If there is designated areas, such as, a kitchen dining area use it. By eating your meals in the designated area means that everyone is on the same page. So regardless of the smell, the dining area is used specifically to contain any aromas.

BEING SICK

What I have found is many people will come to work with a cold or flu or some kind of illness. Of course, it is inevitable that all of us, at some point will get a cold or flu, but some people are sick more frequently than others are. These individuals also seem to get any bug that is in the vicinity just as if they are a bug magnet of some kind.

Here is the reality. When you go to work when you are sick you spread it or whatever you have all over the workplace like the coffee pot or coffee machine, fridge, counters, printers/copiers , filing cabinets, file folders, telephones, door handles, washrooms and so on. This in turn gets your colleagues and management and others sick. The bug lives in the office until practically everyone gets it.

On top of this, when being sick your energy is low; your decision making is off balance, your quality of work, memory and efficiency are much lower than your normal level. So your overall performance is just as you feel, under the weather. Also by staying at work instead of resting you are extending your recovery period which doesn't have any benefit.

Alternatively, as you stay at home when you are sick you prevent spreading the illness; your fellow coworkers aren't pissed off at you for bringing it to the work place; many coworkers don't frown at you instead they have a high regard for you and respect you for preventing the spread of the sickness.

The moral of the story is stay at home when you're sick, since it's an ethical thing to do; it shows common courtesy and besides no one likes you to be sick around the office especially the senior VPs, CEO or any other executive management and your colleagues. Additionally, you are an employee, you have twelve or more sick days per year that are paid. Why not use them, get paid and relax while being sick so you can get well again in a timely manner. Besides I would only guess your children are sick too and it would be a wonderful time to take care of them and spend some quality time together.

YOUR EMPLOYEE REVIEW

Most of you will be subject to an employee review. This is usually conducted yearly, bi-yearly or quarterly by your immediate supervisor or your boss. The review process usually takes about an hour. This one-on-one session is essential because it is an assessment of you at the work place. The assessment will cover items such as, your future outlook, expectations, your progress, goals and also allows you to voice your opinion about your career and the workplace. These reviews in fact provide you with important feedback about yourself that you will not receive anywhere else.

Feedback you receive reveals things about you like:

- How well you conduct yourself
- How you like your job
- The quality of work you do

- How well you perform and deliver what's expected of you

- How well you get along with others and interact

- Your co-workers observations about you and work performance

- If you are a team player

- What your strengths and weaknesses are

- Your career path expectations, goals and interests

- What skills you would like to attain

- Where you need to improve and your plans are for improvement

- Work attendance, at your job, at gatherings, meetings, and other company events, etc.

Feedback received during reviews is from the outside world. In other words, it allows us to see ourselves how others see us. This means, it's an observation from your boss or supervisor and can also include a 360 review from multiple co-workers. This information tells us how our manager and others view us, in respect to our overall work performance and how well we interact with colleagues. Your review allows you to voice your concerns, problems, and opinions you have about your department, the company, processes, co-workers, and about your job. However, be aware that some managers and even co-workers may be biased.

Therefore, the feedback and outcome can also be unfair that is negative and can be painful which should be acknowledged but not completely discarded. I say this because even though it may appear like biased information, there still are some truths within the mix. In this situation, it is your duty to gather solid evidence to support the truth to exonerate the biased feedback and review results. Productive employee reviews should be positive for any employees, colleagues and even your boss or supervisor.

Healthy and professional reviews provide feedback which is neutral, supportive and very constructive. The main objective of employee reviews are not to belittle or intimidate employees but to coach and help employees improve their performance and reach or exceed their career goals and expectations.

Feedback is the most enlightening information you will have in regard to yourself. The information should be used as a metric to measure you as a person and employee. The information whether it is positive or negative, is still about you. Most importantly, feedback is not found everywhere and when you have access to it, listen and take note.

The reason is feedback allows you to learn about your strengths and weakness, what particular deficiencies you may have in regard to skillsets, training, attitude, approach and self-improvement. Feedback provides awareness so you can make positive changes in your life. This includes adding new skills, improving your strengths and weaknesses, or eliminating other deficiencies you may have. This is all in an effort to place you on a future road to success.

BE PUNCTUAL

Another best practice I found is, to be punctual by being at work a little early before starting. This provides you with time to get settled, make a cup of coffee, get organized, review your log book, prepare for your day or shoot the breeze with other co-workers and to be ready to start work. This extra time can also be beneficial in regard to unforeseen circumstances like traffic problems and delays so you can avoid being late.

Being late to work, or for meetings, presentations and so on is a reflection on you unless of course it is something beyond your control. However if you are continually late for work, I would only guess would be discussed in your employee review. Also this type of conduct will only last a very short period of time until, people get fed up and stop dealing with you and you are disciplined or even lose your job.

Being on time or early on the job or for meetings sends a clear message to your co-workers, managers and supervisors, that you respect others time, are organized and are professional, punctual, take work serious, like your job and are consistent.

COMMUNICATE

We communicate at the workplace in a number of different forms such as, verbal, email, texting, face to face, skype, go-to-meeting, telepresence, body language and telephone. Communication skills by far are one of the most important and are the key to developing a professional presence as a leader or with your managers, supervisors and colleagues. Communication is at the heart of expressing yourself, networking and developing work relationships.

Many of us communicate at the workplace but is it effective communication we use or have? Effective communication is a bi-directional process or being able to speak and listen to others. Being effective means that we have the ability to speak clearly, and concisely to co-workers on any level so they can understand our point of view. It also includes being able to effectively listen to others so we can understand them as well. By being able to communicate effectively avoids confusion, mix-ups, frustration, conflicts and also enhances trust, decision making and problem solving.

We need good communication at the workplace so we can, express our opinion during an employee review session, to provide ideas in brain storming sessions, verbalize observations about health and safety concerns, be a whistle blower on theft or co-worker misconduct, abuse and so on.

Another valuable point to mention is when working with colleagues on a project or assignment. When involved in these kinds of situations communication is crucial. The reason is that all people involved on the project group or team need to know and to be informed at all times about work related items, especially in regard to schedule, milestones, costs and deadlines.

Communication is a skill that can be learned by anyone and is the foundation of success in many areas of our lives especially at the workplace. Having open communication is at the heart of successful relationships in the workplace, provides a pathway to higher efficiency, professionalism, understanding and contributing to a team and most importantly to mutual understanding.

Many people communicate but don't communicate effectively so it's up to you to have the capability to and help you pave a successful path to your future.

STRESS

Another most important best practice I have found is dealing with stress that comes with the ups and downs we all face as employees, regardless of what position we hold. Some individuals handle stress better than others; some bring on unnecessary stress into their lives; while others are like a pressure cooker when it comes to stress. Take note that the higher up the career ladder you climb, the more responsibility you have, the more pay but also, MORE STRESS.

Nonetheless, stress is a part of being human, so dealing with it is a must and requires a plan to manage and cope with it. How does stress get into our lives anyway? It enters our lives when certain unexpected events or incidents happen, that makes us feel overwhelmed because we don't have the ability to deal with or control the situation at hand.

For instance, you are driving to the office for an important meeting that starts at 9:00 am. You're being punctual, have left your home at 8:00 am about 30 minutes earlier than usual. As you are driving to work, enjoying your cup of coffee, listening to some music or the news, suddenly the road closes because of a car accident. Now you are sitting on the highway waiting for it to open so traffic can start flowing again. So far, you have been patiently waiting for 30 minutes and finally a police cruiser appears. You are still 25 minutes away from work and need at least another 5 minutes to find parking.

Now you have been waiting for 50 minutes, and traffic isn't moving. You are still waiting for this accident to be cleared and you don't see a tow truck yet. Your stress level is starting to increase and pressure is building since you realize that you are late for the meeting and you must be there because you're the host.

Finally you see some activity of a couple of tow trucks, and for a moment you are relieved, then reality sets in. Now you are becoming very stressed out and angry. After another 20 minutes of waiting, finally vehicles are partially cleared and traffic slowly starts to move. As soon as you see a clear spot in traffic, you step on the gas and speed to work as if you're in the Indy 500. You arrive at the office location and turn into the parking lot. You are about an hour late but you still have to find parking. You are frantically circling around the parking lot looking for a parking spot but can't find one. As you are circling around and around searching, finally, you see a person leaving a parking stall right in front of you. You stop put on your turn signal and wait however; they are taking their time pulling out.

Meanwhile, you are becoming even more stressed and angry with this person for taking their damn time exiting the parking spot so slowly. You are impatient sitting there waiting and waiting for them to leave while you are muttering and cursing at them. They finally leave, and then you park.

You get out of the car; briskly start running to the building, but you forgot your laptop in the car. You run back to the car and grab your laptop. You bolt towards the building again, go through the doors and find the elevator and are on your way to the 32nd floor. You are angry because you're late and you know that people are sitting there waiting for over an hour. You are hosting the meeting, and feel humiliated since you are always punctual and like to be early. You fear that you have damaged your reputation by making everyone wait.

You open the office door and the admin greets you, "Good morning Brenda they're all in there waiting for you." You reply, "Thanks and I'm late". She smiles and says, "Oh, traffic" You sigh, "Yes, traffic". At this point you are exhausted, embarrassed, profusely sweating, in anxiety, angry and stressed-out. Is this the ideal way or condition to be in for a meeting? What kind of meeting will you have? What kind of actions could you taken to prevent this outcome in the first place?

The main point is to have a basic stress management plan which involves strategies for dealing with stress. In this particular scenario of being late and stressed, actions could have been taken beforehand to relieve or even prevent stress, anger, and anxiety from even entering the picture. For example, when seeing that traffic wasn't moving because of an accident, you could have easily picked up your cell phone and called the office. You inform the admin that you would be at least 40 to 50 minutes late due to traffic problems.

This simple action immediately lets you relax, because people in the meeting will know exactly why you are late. Most importantly, you have taken the initiative to inform colleagues you will be late due to circumstances that are out of your control. This in fact allows meeting attendees to do other tasks for the next hour until you arrive. Keep in mind attendees may be booked and the meeting may have to be re-scheduled. Regardless, all of these actions are a positive, since you have shown that you respect others time and have taken responsibility for the situation. Having an action plan and some simple stress strategies can make a world of difference when it comes to changing or turning situations around that prevent, reduce or eliminate our stress.

Having a stress plan is great but first, you have to list all of the things that make you get stressed out in your personal and professional life. List the stress maker items because you have to know what creates stress before you can manage it. Some typical work stress makers usually involve, job loss, procrastination, no cash flow, not meeting deadlines or having unreasonable deadlines, high debt or credit card bills, presentations, heated arguments with coworker, taxes, traffic, being late, workload, complexities, economic downturns, equipment problems, unemployment, layoffs or maybe the job market has tightened, and so on.

Once you've listed your stress triggers, you can produce some corresponding action plans to cope and deal with the particular stress situations. A few simple actions within the plan should reduce or even eliminate the stress and turn a negative situation into a positive one. There are a number of different ways of handling stress, and the steps you take are unique to you because, everyone handles stress differently and has their own triggers. One important point to mention is you should be aware that there are two basic ways to deal with stress.

Handling stress of course depends on the individual, so some people use unhealthy methods of dealing with their stress while others use a healthy approach. Unhealthy methods usually include many vices people have, such as:

- Smoking

- Drinking

- Using illegal drugs

- Binging on junk food, such as, candy, chips, cookies, pastries, and popcorn

- Excessive use of over-the-counter (OTC) drugs such as, sleeping pills, ibuprofen, muscle relaxants, pain killers, gravol, Benadryl, etc. or

- Prescription drugs such as codeine, fentanyl, Demerol, Percocet, methadone or others

None of these unhealthy ways provides a sound means of alleviating stress. Even though those who use them may think they help but in fact they actually increase stress. For instance, when a person uses smoking or other drugs it actually elevates their heart rate higher than it is already. This in turn puts even more stress on their heart and other organs. Keep in mind that smoking, drinking and drugs are the worst things to do in the state of stress, so abstinence would be in your favor.

Other unhealthy ways of dealing with stress can be:

- Procrastinating
- Yelling and screaming
- Getting angry
- Blaming others
- Having a quick fuse
- Becoming verbally abusive to colleagues or others or
- Becoming violent

These are ineffective and don't help with the situation that is creating or causing the stress. Using healthy or positive actions as an alternative actually help combat stress and benefit your body.

Some healthy ways of dealing with stress start with exercise and working out which may sound like it doesn't belong here but it does. Working out and being active before or after work, or having a lunch break walk is essential for dealing with stress. Keep in mind that exercise is not the same as the physical aspects of your job. In other words, having a physically active job is your job, not exercise. Adding exercise to your stress management plan is a start.

Your plan's first element should have a 45 to 60 minute regular exercise routine that you can easily repeat on a daily basis or at least four times per week. To get you motivated, join a gym and use the treadmills, elliptical, weights or other machines that are available. You can also attend group classes, such as, yoga or BodyFlow[3] (preferred), BodyCombat[3], BodyPump[3], RPM[3], BodyStep[3], CXWorx[3], core floor exercises, Pilates, aerobics, or step classes.

Other outdoor routines, may include such activities as, inline skating or rollerblading, running, jogging, walking, cycling, or a combination of…All of these are good exercises to incorporate into your stress management plan. Working out regularly is number one when it comes to handling your stress. The reason is it:

- Reduces stress
- Helps us sleep
- Gives us more energy
- Keeps blood pressure at healthy levels
- Maintains overall fitness

---

[3] Les Mills Classes- usually offered at participating gym facilities

- Prevents weight gain

- Promotes healthy bowel and digestive functions

- Keeps us healthy and

- Burns-off all the bottled up anxiety driven energy we have

Another element to add is having a high fiber balanced diet which is essential for growth and the maintenance of our body. Healthy diets are to prevent weight gain, provide the natural vitamins, minerals and other nutrients we need, gives us energy, prevents illness, keeps our cholesterol in check, and blood pressure at healthy levels. Additionally, it helps us sleep better and improves our bowel and digestive functions.

Another element involves discussing things that are stressful to you. This means talking to people like your spouse, best friend or friends. Speaking to others always helps since it is like a sounding board allowing you to hear your own views and receiving opinions and views of others. Talking it out also assists in coming up with solutions or to bring on awareness of things you didn't know about.

Another item to add is, knowing what your limitations are which involves learning to say no. Many of us try to be the hero by taking on way too many tasks or work all at the same time. This actually results in cultivating stress we create ourselves instead of avoiding unnecessary stress. In this type of situation first we must catch ourselves doing this. Afterwards balance our limits by only taking on as much as we can comfortably handle.

Another plan element to add is in regard to solely taking full responsibility for a situation, or problem. This means that it is not only you that has the full brunt of handling all the stress and responsibility. It's usually a team effort of the department or group that all share the same goal and associated stress.

Another element to add to your plan is in regard to, being willing to make allowances or to compromise since everything you are doing or as a group is not set in stone. As I mentioned earlier, there is no such thing as having solutions only being black or white because there are always many shades of different greys and colors. So being stubborn, or being one that is right all the time doesn't work in the real world and only produces tension and unnecessary stress for you and others.

Another action element to include would be prioritizing your time and workload efficiently. This action plays a very significant role because if you take on too much, you will never have the time or resources to complete the tasks which will create pressure and stress. If you list and prioritize items this helps your direction and focus. This allows you to deal with one item at a time instead of becoming overwhelmed by looking at everything all at once. Make a priority list of the items that have to be completed. Focus on one thing at a time and keep knocking them off the list which helps you avoid confusion and meet deadlines. Again, this is a part of your organizational skills and efficiency.

Another very positive and fruitful action is based on rest and relaxation. In other words, get proper sleep and rest, like 8 hours a day or more. This is very important because, it provides the rest and downtime we need to:

- Maintain our physical health
- Keep us alert and focused
- Provide energy we need
- Give us stability and balance
- Rejuvenate our bodies
- Keep us razor-sharp and
- Maintain our overall mental health

Having inadequate sleep time, results in clouded judgment, emotional based opinions, and changing our overall attitude and outlook. When we become over tired by losing sleep we start to become very emotional and overly sensitive to things that we normally wouldn't be. Being emotional is okay but not over-emotional and too sensitive since at work it could create problems. It's better to get a proper rest, to stay positive, stable and to have an upbeat attitude about work and life.

So far we have seen that some or even many situations tend to create massive amounts of worry and anxiety which all equates to stress. Of course, I am guessing that many of you have heard the saying "stress will kill you" and sadly it will if you don't find some healthy ways of coping with stress. Stress kills since it actually changes our body functions by weakening our immune system so we easily catch colds, flu's or other bugs.

I have worked in the corporate world for over 15 years and have found that many people are always sick and seem to catch every small bug that surfaces anywhere. I have also witnessed people that are only in their late twenties, early thirties and have high blood pressure. Yes, high blood pressure in their late twenties, early thirties. If it's not genetic or hereditary, what the hell are these people going to do when they are fifty if they make it that far?

This in my humble opinion is the result of not dealing with the stress they encounter in their jobs and not having a plan or an effective way of managing their stress. Hey, maybe they think only old people have problems like that? Regardless, if these individuals continue to ignore stress, they will eventually have problems with failing health like, high blood pressure, heart attacks, eye or vision problems, low energy, weakened immune systems, and/or some other major ailments brought on by their unhealthy practices.

Know that stress is inevitable and a part of being human, and most importantly it doesn't discriminate. Any situations or circumstances that arise in your career or in your personal life will generate some kind of stress, so dealing with it is a must.

So far, we have discussed only the basics of stress, coping and handling stress, a few unhealthy and healthy ways people cope with stress but of course there is a lot more to it. The stress plan you devise will be unique to your own needs. The elements that are or should be common to everyone's stress management plan, I feel are regular exercise, healthy diet, rest and relaxation and having a positive mindset.

I can only *stress* that you devise a plan and do some research by going to the following URLs for some more helpful information and tips.

- http://www.helpguide.org/articles/stress/stress-management.htm

- http://www.mayoclinic.org/healthy-lifestyle/stress-management/basics/stress-basics/hlv-20049495

- http://www.fosteringresilience.com/stress_management_plan.php, or

- http://www.gentle-stress-relief.com/stress-plan.html

- http://www.webmd.com/balance/stress-management/stress-management-relieving-stress

ALI-BABA

Don't be an Alibaba which means don't be a thief. Sure many of you are probably sitting there scratching your head thinking...thief... how dare you even suggest that I could be a thief? Well I feel like you do but, people in general don't realize that employee theft at the work place is a very common practice. Some have awareness of theft that is deliberate while others have no awareness.

Some are not aware that simple things they think are just their own stupidity or forgetfulness is not considered theft but in reality it is. I have even done this myself along with probably every person out there. The one common theft I am speaking of is, when you get home after a long day at work, you realize that you have a pen from work, in your pocket or in your purse. This may seem very insignificant or trivial but this is actually considered to be theft. I'm sure the company is not going to prosecute you over a 25 cent pen, but this is still theft.

On the other hand those individuals, who are aware, perform all kinds of theft, such as defraud the company financially, steal equipment, hand tools, power tools, ladders, office supplies, set up accounts using the company's name to get discounts and, setting up supplier accounts with known friends, so they can receive kickbacks from their friend's business and so on.

According to the Jack L. Hayes International's 27th Annual retail theft survey, it states that:

- One out of every 38 employees was apprehended for theft from their employer which is based on data of over 3 million employees

- In 2014, 80,366 employees were apprehended for theft totaling over $66 million dollars with each case averaging $825.36

- To read more about this survey go to the following URL: http://hayesinternational.com /news/annual-retail-theft-survey/

One example of Alibaba I can share stems from working for a field-service. A few weeks after I had left, the company started investigating some theft scam that was happening. The operations manager finally got out of his office and started checking company inventory and physically tracking it down. During this process the manager uncovered a theft scam was happening and it turned out that it was active for a couple years.

This scam was actually worth millions of dollars and included several employees within the company. The scam was played out by three key employees, the base manager, the admin support, and an accounting department employee in head office. Periodically it also included a few employees from some of the local suppliers.

The scam playbook played out like this. The base manager would draw up a purchase order for a piece of equipment such as a drill press. The order would be processed by the admin, and then sent to the accounting department for payment. The accounting employee would pay the false purchase order. The item would be shipped to another address then sold discounted for cash. Then the money would be conveniently distributed between the three employees and at times some external participants.

So as the operations manager was checking inventory it would show a $20,000 drill press on the books. When the operations manager would search for this brand new drill press it wouldn't be there; only the original old drill press. This scam continued with the purchase of millions of dollars of equipment and services that were never fulfilled only the payment and the money. Anyway, the individuals involved were fired and also received a criminal record to boot.

Another example of being an Alibaba wasn't geared to a workplace but to a foreign country when I was working as a technical advisor. First of all in Iran the culture dictated that most people didn't use toilet paper after defecating instead they would do their duty by using their left hand and some water. With this action the culture again stated that eating was done with the right hand while the left hand was usually kept under the table.

The laws in Iran were many, either religious based or judicial that of course, didn't exist in the western world. However, one of these laws of probity was in regard to dealing with Alibaba types. The penalty for being caught and charged for stealing was to have the thief's left-hand cut-off.

The symbolism of this practice is twofold. One, when removing the thief's left hand it would show the public that this person was a thief. The second aspect, forces the thief to eat and do their duty with the same hand, thus humiliating and disavowing their dignity.

If you have the urge to steal, money, equipment, supplies, or just the act of doing it, DON'T! The best practice is to not steal and it's in your best interest to go get some help from a mental health care specialist like a psychologist or psychiatrist about your urges to steal. Stealing is never in your best interest and is destructive behavior. When you steal and get arrested you will be charged by the court of law, have a criminal record, and lose your job. In other words, don't be an Alibaba because with a record it's very difficult to find decent employment.

THEY ARE ONLY PEOPLE

I find that a lot of people in the workplace become speechless, scared, nervous and panic when in the presence of VPs, CEOs, Presidents or other high level management or even owners of the company. The reason is these individuals feel inadequate and intimidated by the management executives.

Why do they feel like this? Having low self-esteem and confidence plays a major role and these individuals generally place these management executives on a pedestal of some kind. Therefore, feel that executives are above them, better people, smarter, richer, and more powerful than they are. Hey some even are afraid that they will say the wrong thing, fumble, or get fired, which in truth is absurd.

Sure these executives may have a status in the company hierarchy but the truth is they are human just like anyone else. These executives have worries, anxiety, frustrations, fears, families, and a spouse like most of us. They may be divorced, but still pay bills, have aches and pains and just like anyone else like a good laugh. So if you believe that they are somehow above you and others guess again. The reason I say this is it's the unrealistic views people have of these executives that creates the panic or awkwardness. If you view these individuals at basic human levels you'll find they are very nice people and very easy going. I say this since I found that the higher up the ladder people are the more open and pleasant.

For example, I can remember six of us going to the head office to attend a meeting for signing an international employment contract. The company we were working for was a big publicly-traded company with gross revenues of over $250 million a year. The meeting was in a large boardroom on the 27th floor and the entire executive management team of the company was in attendance. The team consisted of the CEO/President, Executive VP, and VPs of North American Sales, International Sales, World Operations, Finance, Health and Safety, as well as, a couple corporate lawyers.

The meeting started with a briefing on the work location, country laws, logistics, risks, and then to sign the employment contracts. While the VP of International Sales was speaking he ended with details about the local laws such as it was against the law to approach or speak to any women. At the end of his speech he asked if there were any concerns. I in my early twenties thought there was and asked, "If it's against the law to approach women what if they approach me?" The room went quiet for a couple of seconds, then the CEO looked at me with a smile and said, "Hey Renstone didn't they tell you we are going to clip your nuts before we send you?" The whole room burst out in uncontrollable laughter. When the meeting came to an end all contracts were signed and a month later we all commenced work in the Middle East location.

Another example I have is when I was working for a large commodity transportation company. While in the coffee room, I would unknowingly speak to many senior management executives, and conversations were on a human level. Human level doesn't mean that this person is like your close friend and you are spilling all your problems on the executive or the CEO, but about things that may be obvious.

While grabbing a cup of coffee a VP came in. Of course, at the time I didn't know this person was an Executive VP but I could see that their hand was bound with a bandage. I asked about what happened to their hand and they opened up and told me the story. It was unfortunate but they had an injury while cycling that damaged their hand function. The sad part that was in question pertained to after the healing process was complete. They didn't know if their hand functions would ever be normal again. I spoke to this Executive VP on a human level, shared empathy and feelings with some hope about the mobility and functionality of their hand after it heals. Afterwards, this VP knew who I was and would say good morning if we crossed paths, or even stop, poke their head into my office to make a comment that was, funny or just a greeting.

So, there is no reason to feel intimidated by any executive team members, but if you are stuck in an elevator together alone, I would keep any talk to a minimum and very shallow, like saying good morning, or comment about weather or a sports game. Also just because you are in an elevator with anyone alone doesn't mean that you are obligated to say something. You can always avert conversation by using your cell phone or if you don't know what to say don't say anything just smile.

This best practice is about not feeling intimidated or awkward when it comes to executive management personnel. This will take some work on your part to realize they are only people and to not place them on a pedestal but have respect for the high-stress positions they do hold and carry out.

THE FOLLOWERS AND DOERS

There are two kinds of people in the workplace, followers and doers. The followers are those who follow others and wait to be given work; doers are those who under their own initiative, search for work to do and complete it. Well, there is no right answer because either type of person is acceptable.

The exception, here is, if you are a follower and waiting for someone to give you something to do that's okay. However, if you are sitting there waiting without the need to find something to do, well that is a different story altogether and frowned upon. This inaction taken by the employee sends a message of being a procrastinator, lazy, and one who doesn't care to do their job. They would rather do personal stuff instead until being told to or directed to do some tasks. This kind of attitude is not in anyone's best interest and it makes it very difficult to get a different position or promotion within the organization or may result in job loss.

The preferred employee is a "doer" who under his or her own initiative acts on work without waiting for an assignment. Also doers are those that gladly accept extra work that helps their supervisor or team progress. Doers are go-getters that cannot sit idly by while doing nothing; they must have a focus, direction and most importantly live to be productive. I personally am a doer and can't stand not having a stack of work waiting for me to get through it. If I don't have stacked work I start to question whether there is enough work to stay employed or to wonder what is happening with the future of the company.

For instance, when working for a pipeline service company I was hired as a field electronics engineering technologist. I was responsible to operate, maintain and repair high-tech instruments used for inspecting pipelines. I was trained by using an on-the job training process, then I was selected to be trained on the newest and most sophisticated instrument the company had. At the time this was the most technologically advanced instrument of its kind in the world. I was very excited and trained under the senior scientist and other development personnel who actually designed the instrument.

During this training I began to document all the processes, software user manuals and operating procedures then started to transfer the information into formal, operating, maintenance, repair, troubleshooting procedures and work instructions. In the end this documentation I created covered all aspects about the instrument and was used for training personnel. This was all under my own initiative; because no one asked me to do this, I simply felt it was necessary to help myself retain information but also, to benefit other colleagues. After breaking the international market with this instrument family, I received a pay raise and a new role within the company.

THE POSITIVE SIDE OF THINGS

Having a positive attitude is a bonus since people who are smiling and happy attract like-minded people. People in general are attracted to bubbly, happy people and like being in their presence, working with them in the same department, group, or project or on the same team. Positive people generally show they are confident, flexible, have low stress, very few worries and low anxiety.

Besides being positive, staying positive regardless of the situation at hand shows people you have a good grip on handling and dealing with stress. Being positive builds a friendly stress free zone that encourages high productivity, alliances, teamwork, free thinking, open discussions, comradery, team and relationship building, humor and more. Generally many people avoid working with opposite types who emit negative vibes and have head strong attitudes.

On the other hand, those who are negative minded, grumpy, bitching and complaining all the time also attract like-minded people. Generally, I have found that these individuals usually crash and burn, meaning they end up quitting their job and move on. The mindset of these individuals is filled with high expectations. This means the salary they are paid or the tasks, or company policies, procedures, equipment, environment, or even coworkers are never good enough for this person. In truth, regardless of where they go or transfer to, it will never be good enough.

So, it is in your best interest to be upbeat, positive about work and life since it helps live a better life. Keep in mind that many people are negative because of their unreasonable expectations about work and their life in general. These people have, at some point in their life, removed the words, "gratitude or being grateful" from their vocabulary. They focus on what they don't have and have forgotten to be grateful for all of the wonderful things they do have in their lives. So, it's all up to you to decide whether you would like to look at work and life, as the glass being half full or half empty. All I can suggest is being positive and happy is a lot easier at work and in life because you will shine at work and be popular with many.

IT'S A MISTAKE

I found throughout my whole career that many employees, especially management cannot admit to making mistakes at the workplace. These individuals can or may make wrong decisions or mistakes and errors, which may result in:

- Losing clients or employees

- Damaging the company's reputation

- Equipment or system failures

- Producing project overruns

- Being over budget on projects or programs

- Raising health and safety risks

- Causing delays on projects and deliverables

- Generating a huge make-work project that loses the company a lot of money

- Forming and contributing to a negative frustrating work environment

Regardless of what it is, errors are always hidden by these so called infallible individuals. Unless of course the errors are impossible to hide or cover-up or to put it another way they are, "caught red-handed". Even in this circumstance, some management will still deny responsibility for their mistakes. Regardless, this conduct is deceitful and precarious in nature and at times includes blaming others for their mistakes. Moreover, this behavior clearly illustrates the individual is, lying by omission, unreliable, not trustworthy, and has no integrity. These actions also lead to the individual destroying their work relationships and losing their job not for the mistake but for lying. Is it worth it? I say no. By hiding errors it only amplifies the problem caused by the mistake or error.

When it comes to human error, even this information is purposely excluded by the infallible employee. This makes it is very difficult to determine the real problem, fault, or cause of the original event because of the information gap. Furthermore, it makes it merely impossible to formulate an accurate assessment and to make correct decisions. So, any corrective actions may have no effect on the situation because it may not be a design flaw or, execution plan fault but only human error.

As a best practice always take full ownership of your mistakes, screw-ups and errors because it shows you are only human. Besides it also shows you are not perfect, take responsibility for your mistakes, have integrity, and show strength because you are not afraid of admitting to any mistakes or errors that have been made. In fact, there are no excuses to justify hiding errors because all people make errors, mistakes and screw shit up. Besides, I found it doesn't matter how experienced, educated, skilled, or specialized, anyone is they always make mistakes, so be proud to own them it's a part of being human.

PERFECT!

Perfect! Yes being perfect or a perfectionist actually works hand-in-hand with trying to be infallible which both are not possible nor are they in your best interest.

Striving to be perfect or looking for perfection is impossible because human beings are not perfect, so it is inevitable to have flaws, make mistakes and errors, typos, omissions, forget, and screw shit up, make wrong decisions, break stuff, drop things, knock things over, add too much and on and on.

So unless you are superhuman or from another planet you are not perfect and never will be so, accept that you and everyone around you makes errors and mistakes regardless if they won a Nobel prize, have awards for excellence, medals of honor, presidential medal of freedom, or are a genius.

Perfectionists are trying to achieve what is unachievable but of course trying to get as close to perfect as possible, which to them is only frustrating, exhaustive and annoying. Unfortunately, if you cannot stop this and it's up to you to seek out professional help for your compulsive behavior. Trying to be perfect is very exhausting and wastes precious time and energy that could be spent on other things.

Being perfect is only for those entities or things that are, but not people, even though I have met my fair share of "perfect a-holes."

WORKING AT THE RUMOR MILL

Working at the rumor mill refers to being involved with the rumors and gossip that circulate within the workplace.

The deceptive information usually focuses on a co-worker, management, department or group or the company. These worthless reports are usually invented by uninformed and/or biased individuals or can also be accurate information that was changed and distorted by word of mouth.

Generally, employees create this misinformation because of their own bias, opinions, frustrations, anger, jealousy, envy, distortions, revenge, or speculation. This act can also be carried out because of a change or decision made by the company, like layoffs, demotion, career stagnation, no pay raises or it may be just some off the wall dark humor.

Rumors can also be derived by original and accurate information that was leaked by someone in the know. However, shortly after the information is released to someone, it is clobbered by word of mouth as it spreads around the work place. This results in the original information being distorted or adlibbed which has transformed sound information into something that has no merit.

Rumors can and will create and stimulate many people into believe things that are untrue about the company or its employees. This in fact can significantly influence co-worker moral, productivity, attitudes and beliefs. This impacts employees by creating a negative atmosphere about the company, job security, layoffs, thus inducing fear and anxiety around the workplace. This negative information can affect employees by significantly changing their attitude and flipping it by 180 degree thus placing them on a path of hating their job and making them eventually quit. Do you want this to happen to you? I would say no.

As an employee it is in your best interest to AVOID getting involved with any misinformation, gossip, rumors or any other skewed information delivered by unreliable sources. The most important thing you can do is to pay strict attention to information which is only relayed by reliable sources such as, senior management, your supervisor or manager. Reliable information is formal and circulated throughout the company via email, meetings, town halls, and so on. So, as an employee it is your duty to confront and report these individuals who spread misinformation because they are there to ruin people's lives.

ONLY YOU

This best practice is simple because it refers to being you. Be you anywhere you are, since when others try being someone they're not, it's blatant to everyone else. Being yourself means that you don't have to make an effort because it's all natural and seamless. Being yourself means that you accept yourself in entirety that includes all your imperfections, flaws, mistakes, errors, innate abilities, talents and gifts that are all a part of you. Besides, each person is unique from birth which many don't comprehend and alternatively pursue a multitude of ways of trying to be different or unique.

Don't ever hide yourself for any reason even when there are times when you find it difficult to be yourself. These difficult situations may be because of peer pressure or some of your, opinions, likes, dislikes, passions, beliefs, ideas, or your intelligence differs from others or the group. At times you may be within a group or meeting and be the only one with a brilliant idea or an opinion that stands alone and it's all okay. There are also other times when some people may not be able to grasp nor understand your insightful perspective or forward thinking.

Those who do not grasp the concept or idea may be feeling intimidated by your qualities and talents and in truth there is no reason for it. This may be that some have difficulty with understanding new concepts or changes. In this situation you can explain the concepts or ideas by using another delivery method because all people learn differently. Others may feel that any change is not interesting because they like it the way it is because of the anxiety it creates. When being assertive about your ideas or concepts do not attempt to sway their opinion about your solution, concept or procedure. Let them decide for themselves.

Being yourself allows you to be unique, to have autonomy and to be an individual that is a part of the group that has their own mind. You are a contributor to the group and company. Besides there is nothing wrong with being who you are, in fact it's natural.

YOUR ATTENDANCE

As an employee your attendance is very important for any kind of company function, whether it is a Christmas or retirement party, team discussion, or employee review. Other crucial meetings you should attend are departmental, health and safety, weekly, strategic, brainstorming, and especially town halls.

Your attendance is a measurement of your interest, participation, enthusiasm, being a team player, and how dedicated you are, in all aspects of the organization. Attendance is in your best interest, to go to every meeting and function, and participate, because your boss and senior management depend on your presence as a part of their group or team.

If you're absent it reflects your lack of enthusiasm and interest which also may be interpreted as having a negative attitude about the company. Your absence is noted by your boss and senior management. This in fact can affect your chances of, being promoted, pay raises, good performance reviews, or any current or upcoming opportunities that may become available. Attend every meeting regardless, since it's about your future and reputation.

KISS ME

When speaking to colleagues make sure you are very clear and concise. There is nothing worse than someone who tries to impress others by exercising their high-level or very technical vocabulary to show people how smart they are, when in fact it shows the opposite. At times when using a high level vocabulary, it makes simple conversation very complex and loses the participants. Consequently this is defeating the whole purpose of relaying your message.

In my understanding those individuals who have a high level and/or very technical vocabulary should be able to align according to the audience. The reason is when speaking or writing to anyone, you are trying to convey a message that all listeners, readers or participants can comprehend. This is the reason why magazines and newspapers are written at about grade 8 to 10 reading level of English. Of course, there is a place and time for using high vocabulary or technical jargon which is when addressing an audience of specialists, engineers, medical doctors, or physicists, etc.

When things are complex, it can create confusion, mistakes and errors, frustration, fear, anxiety, misunderstandings, misinterpretation, offend some people, make people feel stupid or inadequate or to have them give up altogether. This in turn results in performing work incorrectly, decreases worker productivity, and reduces efficiency and quality.

Keeping things simple such as procedures, explanations, and communication is a benefit since it avoids people being confused or having misunderstandings. The simpler things are, the better it is. With this in mind, having everyone understand the information results in helping things flow smoother, increases efficiency, quality and productivity and employee morale.

Consequently, the acronym, KISS was formulated which stands for, "Keep It Simple, Stupid". When using this formula regardless of whatever you are trying to accomplish, everyone wins!

THERE IS NOTHING ELSE

There is nothing else refers to the, "truth"; since the truth is all there is. So tell the truth because lying is not in your best interest whether it's personal or work oriented. Lying is to no one's benefit, because it misleads people, is dishonest, deceitful, and hurtful while destroying the liars integrity. When a person is lying it means that other lies must be concocted to cover the original lies. Then those additional lies must be covered by even more lies and as time passes, lies are being produced at an exponential rate. Besides, who in the world keeps track of all the lies and who can remember all of the lies that were stacked upon each other? This only ends by the liar eventually being caught since it's merely impossible to account for all of the lying. Besides, you will be labelled as, "Liar, Liar, Pants on Fire!"

When the person is caught, saying a simple sorry doesn't have much merit and doesn't undo what has been done. Lying damages the person's trustworthiness, integrity, reputation and usually results in, career stagnation with no chance of advancement, demotion, or even job loss.

So, keep in mind that when you tell the truth, there is no need to try and remember what the cover up was or the story or any other lie or series of lies that were told and to who...because with truth..."There is nothing else."

YOU'RE NOT ALONE

As an employee you will always be working with other colleagues, groups and teams at any workplace. The number of employees at an organization will vary in size and corresponds to the company's financial and market size. Within the group of co-workers lies a very diverse mix of people who all have their own individual qualities, strengths, weaknesses, personalities, and other traits. These diversities that make up the group of colleagues consist of languages, education level, sexual orientation, age, gender, race, religion and culture. Even with such complexity, all employees work together to meet company goals but still experience difficulties.

Regardless of the diversity, I have found some co-workers feel that they are alone in their workspace. By this I am referring to how employees ignore other co-workers or are oblivious to anyone else being in the vicinity except for them. This kind of behavior portrayed by employees consists of being discourteous, disrespectful, and indifferent to other co-workers and is a perfect formula for setting up many problems. Consequently, these self-centered actions result in creating conflicts, frustration, discomfort, disruption, disputes and anger amongst fellow colleagues in the workplace.

The situations I have seen and experienced first-hand usually happen when sharing an office or being in an office cube farm, or making meals while at work. For instance, when these kinds of self-absorbed individuals are in a cube farm they have no awareness of its structure and characteristics.

A basic cube farm is a simple structure with small walls that are on average about 5 feet tall and interconnect to provide basic work areas or cubicles in the smallest space possible. This means that everyone is clustered together into a relatively small space. These cubicles provide some kind of quasi-visual privacy for each person but this depends on the design and layout of the farm. In other words, being in a cube is like being surrounded by glass walls with no doorway because everyone can see everything you do, hear all that you say, see any behaviors or habits you may have and how clean and organized you keep your workspace.

With that in mind, people walking by can just look into the cube through the main entrance to see behaviors or habits of the occupier, or any pictures or material hanging and more. For instance, if you have a habit of picking your nose, or something even more disgusting, everyone around you or walking by knows. So privacy isn't a part of your workspace so how you conduct yourself really matters especially when it comes to your sounds.

Another detail about cube structure is they are not sound proof. So everyone can hear any sound coming from any cube. For instance, if someone is speaking using their normal voice level everyone in the farm can basically hear what is being said whether the individuals are on the phone, or in face to face conversation. If for some reason you get irritated or upset and start raising your voice, the whole floor will hear you. For these situations book a meeting or break-out room to be behind closed doors so others are not disrupted. If you need to have a discussion and no rooms are available, go for a walk or a coffee outside the workplace to avoid disrupting your colleagues. Don't forget about the other random sounds that can be heard.

Bodily functions also play a role in producing sounds, such as burping, sniffling, coughing and sneezing. If these functions are frequent they may become disruptive and may even upset, disrupt or disgust people. So if you are continuously coughing, sneezing and sniffling, it suggests you have a cold and then my question would be... why are you at work in the first place? Nonetheless, if its allergies causing sniffles and sneezing then there are many remedies to minimize the symptoms, such as, over the counter or herbal allergy pills, or salt water rinsing using a Neti-pot.

Another bodily function like stomach gurgles, burping and breaking smelly wind, is embarrassing and awkward for most, even though it's a natural function of the human body. Gas is usually created by the types of food we eat, such as beans, sweet peas, donuts, lentils, and any sugar based food that have fructose or lactose and carbohydrates. To avoid these situations, heading to a washroom to break wind is the first choice. However, if gas is a problem then there are also OTC and herbal remedies and food considerations. For more information about controlling gas go to the following URL:

http://www.iffgd.org/symptoms-causes/intestinal-gas/tips-on-controlling-gas.html

Another distractive behavior is some people perform basic hygiene functions like flossing their teeth, trimming their finger nails, painting their toenails or fingernails, brushing their hair, spraying perfume or using an electric razor. Of course any of these are going to create noise or odors and be on display for passersby and all cube farm personnel. So, instead of doing these things at your cubical do it at home before coming to work or go to a washroom. When painting finger or toenails, this is a very strong odor and violates the scent free zone policies that companies have in place.

Other unsettling habits people have are, like talking to themselves, mumbling, tapping pens or fingers and toes or shaking their legs, or other movements which create noise. These are anxiety based actions and the person doing them has no awareness of their actions but those who are in the same area have full awareness. This again will create frustration and disruption amongst colleagues in the area around you. If you can't catch yourself doing these actions, and stop the behaviors, then go to your doctor and ask for some help.

Other things that come to mind are music, radio, office phones or cell phone ringers, computer settings for email arrival and so on. These are also disturbances that affect the whole farm. As far as music, some people use it to motivate themselves and can function great with music blaring in their ears, while others cannot.

So when you are listening to music, don't use a speaker on the computer, tablet or any other device. You can use earphones which will reduce the sound of the music. However, if the volume is turned up loud, some earphones do not block sound so everyone close to the person can actually hear the music being played.

Using music also goes hand in hand with singing, humming, bouncing, and tapping toes, pens and other objects which are all annoying and disruptive. The only suggestions I have are abstinence or to keep your music low and don't bounce around and make other noises. As far as telephones, put the ringer on vibrate, and any notifications on your cell phone or computer should be at zero volume, because all of these things create disturbances with your co-workers.

Another aspect is a co-worker at any time can look over cube walls as long as they are tall enough. When a person is gazing over the walls this poses as a different problem altogether in that the cube occupant has no awareness of someone looking at them from above. I find this behavior to be very creepy and disturbing. I compare it to someone that is standing there watching you sleep or something. Of course, this creepy scumbag will probably start some gossip about your habits. So keep any of your habits to yourself like do them in the washroom. If you do catch someone peeking over your cubical walls, report them to your manager or supervisor immediately. This person is violating you and your space, besides the thought of it is alarming and repulsive.

All of these types of noises and behaviors are very disruptive to the entire farm or office. The disruption is not only based on behavior with no awareness of others being in the vicinity but also completely forgetting about the open concept environment of no privacy, no solid walls and sound proofing. Of course, the office area noises should be discussed between office or cube farm personnel to achieve an environment that is quiet and stable for everyone.

I stress this since if you don't deal with your disruptive behaviors and habits you could end up losing your job. In other words if you continue to disrupt everyone around you, their productivity drastically drops or they can't do their work and it's because of you. After discussing all these disruptive behavior about sharing space it reminds me of a few shared office experiences I have had.

Two Different Jobs

The person I shared an office with was a nice courteous person with awareness of someone else being in the office, but this person's job function as compared to my function was entirely different. This I felt was a poor decision by management to have us share an office because I required a quiet area to think and to perform my job tasks while this other person was carrying out a technical support function. In a support function, this colleague was helping, training and coaching people on the phone for almost 8 hours a day. This was so disruptive that I had to notify my manager that I couldn't share the office with this colleague due to the person's job function. Since I was holding this office for a couple of years already, this person had to vacate and of course took the whole ordeal personally. In truth it had nothing to do with it because it was merely a conflict of both of our job functions.

Not One Thread

Another example of sharing an office was with a colleague who held a position that required being on the telephone occasionally, which was okay for me, and most of the job function was working on the computer. However, in the second week this person became completely oblivious to someone else in the office and didn't have one thread of awareness or courtesy of sharing an office.

Their behaviors included, talking to me excessively, asking technical questions they should have known, singing and humming while working, pen and finger tapping, or listening to music then taping pens, fingers and other objects. I confronted this colleague about their disruptive behavior and it stopped for about a day or two, and then started all over again. Also while on the phone this co-worker in a rage would start yelling at the top of their lungs at the other person on the phone. This colleague was oblivious disruptive behavior and anyone else being in the office. People in the vicinity could even hear the yelling. As always, this behavior was justified in their own mind. After a couple weeks, I had this colleague removed and of course they too took it personally. This reminds me of a shared office situation with both of us doing the same job function but the problem had only one solution.

Temperatures Rise

In this shared office experience, the problem involved room temperature. First of all let me explain some room temperature facts. I found that having the temperature of a room too high will always play a major role in, dry eyes, sweating, making people sleepy or creating other discomforts which affects a person's productivity and may even make them irritable. On the other hand if the work area or office temperature is kept at 70° F to 75° F (21° C to 24° C) this is a moderate temperature used in almost every workplace. This means in this range it will keep you and your colleague awake, comfortable, your eyes will not be dry and will prevent any discomfort. If the temperature is slightly cool for a person, they can always put on a sweater. Even though this temperature range is a standard used by almost all companies, this is how the shared office experience I had played out.

First my co-worker was about 6 feet tall, weighed in at about 90 pounds and was an unhealthy weight almost anorexic. This person required a minimum room temperature of 98° F (37° C) just to feel comfortable in the office. To me this was absolutely unreasonable since most people can be comfortable at 69° F to 73° F (21° C to 23° C). Of course, there are exceptions to what a comfortable temperature is based on where you live and the climate.

For the most part, many people including myself cannot work in a high temperature like the one my office mate required. I was profusely sweating, uncomfortable, had dry eyes, nose and lips and my productivity was almost zero. I couldn't work in this environment. This was a mistake management had made by matching two people together in an office with one requiring an abnormally high temperature. In fact, this person would be impossible to match with anyone unless matched with someone similar. This temperature difference of 30° F made it absolutely impossible to find a compromise or any solution except for moving this person to a separate office. I have never had a problem with temperature until this situation came to roost.

Prior to these episodes I shared office space many times before without problems. In fact I shared an office with a colleague for over three years and never had a problem. Before that I shared an office with four people and so on. Generally as long as people follow shared office etiquette there usually isn't a problem. Well, except once and it was quite funny actually.

I was sitting at my desk and carrying out an online webinar based training session. I was using my computer, microphone and shared screen to relay the information and perform the tasks. While I was in the middle of the webinar, my colleague who sat behind me suddenly received an important phone call and started speaking quite loud. In fact it was so loud that I couldn't continue and had to mute the microphone, to tell my colleague to shut up. Of course, my colleague was feeling somewhat, embarrassed and with a red face apologized. Overall this was a successful share situation because both people had common courtesy and awareness of the other person and had a conscience. So having one incident in over three years is minor.

The last shared office ordeal was when I was working for a large change management project. This situation entailed having four people crammed into an office space so small that, you could only fit four desks into the office. This left enough space to rotate your chair and have just enough room to walk in and out. This I thought was a situation that might have some problems. Actually it didn't at all and in fact, worked out better than any other shared office situations I have encountered. The reason it worked was we were all on the same page, were courteous to each other and were working as a team exchanging knowledge, and working together to achieve a common goal. In this situation it was an excellent match by the management!

COMMON COURTESY

As far as office etiquette and common courtesy goes, this should be in your best interest and is a best practice. The reason for this is so important because you are never alone, nor does everyone share the same viewpoints you have about food, noise, music, and disruptive behavior, etc. When a person is oblivious to the work environment and people around them, their behaviors can and will disrupt and affect one or many of the co-workers in the area. This means this person is intruding their co-worker's space; altering their environment and they in turn lose the ability to control their own work space.

This type of behavior of course directly impacts co-workers overall work performance, by affecting their productivity, attitude, work quality, efficiency, and morale. The most important message here is when a person or people are disruptive, this in reality means that person is, "preventing others from doing their job or substantially reducing their productivity". This has huge ramifications for those who disrupt and are reprimanded accordingly. The outcome may result in a warning, suspension, mandatory therapy or even being fired. Again all it takes is one bad apple to ruin the bunch.

I can't emphasize this enough. It's in your best interest to have awareness of co-workers in your surroundings, to be courteous to colleagues, to follow all company policy and always put yourself in other people's shoes first before acting on anything. This is so you can grasp the impact it will have on other people. If you can't seem to stay within the rules or policies, or to control your behaviors, get some professional help. The reason is it will be difficult to stay employed when having unacceptable disruptive behaviors and inability to follow company policies at the work place.

PERSONAL STUFF

This best practice involves personal stuff. I am talking about, employees doing their personal stuff when they are at work and I found that many spend unreasonable amounts of time doing it.

Some basic personal stuff is like making appointments such as, dentist, doctor, spa, car maintenance or repairs, or hairdresser, house repairs or maintenance and so on. Other personal things involve such items as, chatting with friends on the phone, cell phone texting, writing letters, personal faxes, printing personal things on the color printer, doing google searches on items they are interested in, shopping online, and sending emails, and so on. Using company time is unacceptable. However; there are some exceptions because some personal items cannot be done at any time except during core hours.

Some situations arise that offer no alternative but to act on them during work hours and those in my humble opinion are acceptable. To spend less than a half hour during work on these items is what I consider reasonable if you have already made an attempt during your lunch hour or breaks and were unsuccessful. The reason for keeping personal tasks to a minimum of course is quite simple. As an employee you are paid to perform work related tasks listed in your job description and not your personal ones. Regardless, many people spend a good part of their day or week on their own personal agenda. This behavior will be revealed in their productivity, and efficiency but most importantly will result in being questioned in their employee review about their declining work performance. How do you answer to this in the review when the IT department has proof of your online personal activity and purchases, etc.?

There are other circumstances in our personal lives we may have to deal with like family matters, divorce, litigation, accidents, or deaths and so on. However, dealing with such items may demand a lot of our time. These personal situations of course are unfortunate and the employer will accept an employee using a reasonable amount of company time to sort personal matters but there are limitations and alternatives.

At times some personal circumstances are upsetting and cannot be sorted in a reasonable amount of time and in fact can require days, weeks, months or even years to resolve. Even in these kinds of conditions employees still try to juggle their personal lives at work. When having complex problems, it's in the employee's best interest to take time off using floater, sick and/or holiday days in order to sort their personal problems that require excessive time.

However, there are instances when personal problems arise that are far too complex, and overwhelming or to cope with, that require the employee to take a leave of absence or even quit. I personally experienced it with the loss of my daughter. It was too devastating, overwhelming and very difficult to cope with. I walked straight out of the office, without a care about anything, didn't give notice, explain my circumstance, nor did I ever look back. I was completely dysfunctional for over a year. Would the 2-3 days of bereavement time-off help? No, not even close.

So the moral of the story here is to deal with your personal items on your own time. Unfortunately, if you have a very complex problem with too much to deal with it can result in:

- Severely reduced job performance

- Finding it's merely impossible to think clearly

- Easily make mistakes

- Become too emotional

- Having poor judgement and decision making

- Getting fired or laid-off because of company limitations

- Ending up in your manager's office to discuss what is going on with you and your life

The last point is not ideal since it's really no one's business about very personal things you are dealing with. It's in your best interest to acknowledge the problem and then take appropriate action like seeking help, taking time off, a leave of absence which may save your job. Jobs become very important especially when dealing with certain situations because they actually provide a pillar of focus and help us get through the ordeal, at least most times.

COMMON DUTIES

In any workplace there are common duties that are required by everyone. In truth these duties are just being considerate of others. This courtesy happens in common areas within the office, such as, the kitchen, coffee room, photocopier, printer, and fax machine areas, washrooms and other places.

In the kitchen or coffee area, many employees bring lunch and use any dishes that are available like plates, bowls, and cups in order to eat or drink. When using these dishes, it is in your best interest to take on responsibility and to rinse any dishes you use and place them in the dish washer or wash them. I say this since we are all employees and no one is above being courteous. Other tasks may include, wiping the counter you have soiled, or making a pot of coffee or emptying the coffee grounds, k-cups, or pods.

Other common machines of the office are the fax, copier or printer. If these machines you are using require paper, load paper into the machine. However, if it requires toner or if a problem exists of course contact the admin support and notify them of the problem or the need. When everyone is involved in performing these tasks it makes the workplace efficient. Regardless of where I have worked, I have seen a sign, time and time again, that states, "Please clean up after yourself because your mother doesn't work here"

COUNTING BEANS

Yes this person who counts beans is actually someone you should have doing your tax returns. Having an accountant to do your taxes is a best practice because even if you have a basic income tax return, the accountant can provide you with tax tips and strategies to help you improve and maximize your income tax return and savings.

When using an accountant the IRS, CRA, or HMRC, recognize your income tax return has been prepared by a professional, consider it to be accurate without any errors which most times prevents an audit. Additionally, the fee that you pay the accountant is also tax deductible. With an accountant it is worth every penny because they are professionals and provide sound advice, strategies, save you money and keep you well informed of tax laws.

An accountant is mandatory especially if you have complex income tax returns such as investments, 401 Ks, IRAs, RRSPs, savings accounts, rental properties, capital gains, fringe benefits like a car, golf membership and other benefits.

As a rule of thumb, when hiring an accountant ensure they have a professional designation such as, CGA, CPA or CMA, etc. They must also be registered, current and in good standing with their professional association. If the accountant is not registered or retired and has let their registration slide, this means that they are not current with tax laws nor are they cross examined by their professional association. In other words, if the accountant is not registered find one who is.

You can also check the accountant's status with the professional association they belong to by doing a google search and then contacting the association directly.

GIVE ME A BREAK

"Give me a break" is really referring to breaks that employees have each day like coffee breaks or a lunch break. According to labor law, the employer must provide two 15 to 20 minute breaks per 8 hour workday as well as a 30 minute lunch; however, some companies have one hour lunch breaks. Even though breaks are available, many employees always skip lunch and/or their breaks. They continue to work straight through which in fact is detrimental to their physical and mental health.

Many people don't take breaks because they are in the middle of something, or too busy, have too much work they must get done and so on. While others may feel guilty for taking a break or may be wondering if they will forget what they were working on or are afraid they will lose focus altogether.

People who feel guilty for taking a break base it on false belief, since guilt is learned and one of the most prevalent methods of controlling people. So feeling guilty for taking a break requires the employee to re-think their guilt trip.

Breaks are a part of their job, and law. In fact, there is no reason to feel guilty and besides, employers encourage employees to take breaks.

As far as taking a break while you are knee deep in your work, is up to you. To believe that you will lose your train of thought, or forget what you were doing or lose the drive is again not true. The reason is even when we take a break and shift our focus on something else that is entirely different; our brain is still working on the same stuff we were working on in the office. In fact, once our subconscious has been given a task or a problem to solve, it will be working steadily in the background to analyze and produce a brilliant idea, innovation or solution to whatever we were working on.

When an employee spends prolonged time working at a work station or is performing the same activities, it results in feeling tired because their brain becomes fatigued. Concentration starts to wane, productivity declines, make more mistakes; become forgetful, distracted, confused, anxious or even overly emotional like becoming impatient or irritable. In this state, our quality of work declines and on top of it all our brain tells us we need sleep or in other words we need a break.

Break periods are in place for several important reasons, like to get some nutrients and replenish fluids and to let our brain recuperate. Breaks also allow employees to interrupt their workday, clear their mind, change the pace or switch gears so the employee can have their rest which helps them maintain a higher level of focus and can even boost their energy levels.

Another problem with staying at the same pace and skipping breaks altogether is it promotes ergonomic type injuries due to prolonged time at the work station or performing repetitive physical motions. Also if the workstation is not set up ergonomically then our posture is not correct while sitting at our workstation. This increases the probability of injury or adverse physical effects on our body.

By having extended incorrect posture it will possibly result in slowing blood circulation, affect nerves, soft tissue like tendons, ligaments, fascia, and muscles, etc. This increases the potential for neck pain, upper and lower back pain, shoulder pain and carpal tunnel syndrome. Ask your employer to have an ergonomic assessment of your work station. This will help you to sit with proper posture and avoid any injuries. Even with proper posture take a break regardless of your job function. If your employer doesn't provide you with an ergonomic assessment do it yourself by going to this excellent self-assessment checklist written by Stanford University at the following URL:

https://web.stanford.edu/dept/EHS/prod/general/ergo/PDFs/self_evaluation.pdf

Taking breaks also prevents us from becoming bored or losing interest and day dreaming. Taking breaks to refocus your brain on something completely different usually results in having a fresh view and focus thus increasing productivity, quality of work and attitude.

So, if your job involves working at a computer or doing repetitive physical motions then breaks should be more frequent. In this case have more frequent mini breaks, for two to three minutes at a time at least every hour. Take short breaks regardless even if it involves just a walk to the washroom, to the kitchen to get a beverage or glass of water. During that walk, you are moving around and increasing blood circulation. You can do a number of things which aren't really breaks but break up sitting for prolong periods of time. These are:

- Stretch before you sit down

- Set up a timer on your cell phone to remind you to take a break

- Snack on almonds, seeds, pistachios, or other assorted nuts, fruit or even raw vegetables like carrots, celery, etc.

- Just stand up at your desk, turn around, walk to the door way and look both ways down the hall

- Stand up and do a little stretch

- Walk around the office space, cube or work area then return to your desk

- Print off some or all of what you are working on, which in turn forces you to get up, and pick up your printed material

- Walk over to get some supplies that you may need

- Have a washroom break, or splash some water in your face dry off, or brush your teeth and then return

- When your phone rings stand up and answer the phone

- Get a cup of coffee or a beverage to drink or even wash your cup out

- Empty your individual office recycle bin

These simple actions will allow your body to change stances; make you break the concentration cycle, and stop you from prolonged sitting time while breaking the repetitive cycle.

There are also other consequences connected to prolonged sitting time because time accumulates when you are sitting at home or at the office. Sitting for long periods leads to obesity, in turn increasing blood pressure, blood sugar level, as well as, inducing back, neck, shoulder, buttocks complications and extra pressure to joints and muscles.

If you are required to use a computer at work be sure to wear any prescription glasses you have when looking at your computer screen because without them you have blurred vision, will start having headaches, strain your eyes because they are working harder to focus, thus tiring your eyes and may even physically hurt.

Also when looking at a computer screen for hours always use an eye lubricant, drops or eye gel, because most of us don't blink enough to lubricate our eyes sufficiently. Additionally, if you are living in a dry climate, you should be using a gel or eye lubricant regardless, since dry climate promotes dry eyes. Be sure to lubricate your eyes a few times during your work day. After applying drops keep your eyes closed and let your eyes lubricate. Before using any eye gels, drops or eye lubricants consult your family doctor or optometrist first to find out what lubricants are most effective for dry eyes.

For longer breaks like 15 to 20 minutes or during a 30 minute lunch break, it opens up multiple activities that change your physical stance and to get your mind off of your work. Some things you can accomplish during a 15 to 20 minute break or lunch break can be one of the following:

- Leave the office and walk to a local retailer to get a beverage of some kind at Starbucks, MacDonald's, 7-11, or any other place that's close

- Go for a walk outside around the office building for five minutes or so

- Do a series of stretches

- Go to a colleague's office and grab them to go for a coffee or a short walk outside

- Deal with some personal things via online or by telephone while standing

- Call your spouse while you are walking around outside and have a quick conversation

- Go to a store if they are close by and purchase a few things that you need or would like to read

- Go to the post office to mail something

- Walk to a card shop and pick out a card for your spouse, for their birthday, your anniversary or my favorite, a "Thank You" card for no reason just to tell them you love and appreciate them

- Meditate

The things you can do in a 15 to 20 minute break are endless.

A few points about your lunch period are they will vary from 30 minutes to an hour which provides plenty of time to do many activities. The first point I would like to make is during lunch hour don't over eat so you feel like you are bursting at the seams. I say this because it makes us feel very tired and sleepy due to your body rushing blood to your digestive organs to work on this huge meal. I have found myself many times almost sleeping at my desk because of this.

So eating heavy meals during lunch isn't advisable, but eating many small meals or snacks is a better solution. During lunch there are a whole slew of things to do because of so much time at your disposal. Of course the first thing you should do is eat something that has protein, like a bowl of soup, salad, small wrap or half a sandwich and so on. After that five minute meal, I would suggest going outside or to a park if it's close enough. This lets you enjoy fresh air, sunshine; scenery and some light activity which completely makes you focus on things other than work. Some activities that you can do during your 30 to 60 minute lunch break are such things as:

- Meet a colleague or friend somewhere close and sit outside and have a conversation for a short break

- Go for a 30 minute walk outside in a park or along a river, while chatting with your colleague, friend or spouse, or while listening to your favorite tunes

- Read a book or watch some videos on your PC, cell phone or tablet

- Complete some personal things via online or by telephone that you need done

- You can walk to a bank and get some cash, deposit a check, or pay some bills

- Pick up some dry cleaning

- Get a haircut or trim or shave

- Floor stretches, Pilates, yoga, treadmill as long as you have a gym close by or dedicated room

- Jog, run, inline skate, or skate board, etc.

- Mediate or have a power nap

The activities for lunch hour or coffee breaks are only limited by you. So of course the creativity in activities you can do is all up to you because you are the only one that knows your own workplace and what stores, gyms, parks, walk ways and other shops are close by or within the vicinity.

It is difficult to initially create habits but after a while it will become second nature to take a break and do an activity. It's all up to you to take the first step.

PUT IT IN THE VICE

This best practice is about vices people have since everyone has some form of vice whether it's, smoking, gambling, chocolate, or ice cream, potato chips and so on. The specific vices that I am referring to are the use of drugs or alcohol or both. I am not here to preach to you about your vice or to tell you to quit using drugs or alcohol but rather I would like to provide you with some awareness of the effects of continuous use.

If we use drugs and/or alcohol once every 6 months it doesn't have any adverse effects to our mind and body because of its infrequency. Another point is drinking alcohol socially, is quite popular because many groups of coworkers like to meet up at a pub after work on a Friday, have some finger food and a glass of wine, beer or a cocktail and then go home. This doesn't have any real effect either. However, problems start when some individuals continue to drink more than one serving or repetitively stay at the pub and continue drinking until close or even go home after to continue drinking all night.

This kind of drinking is referred to as recreational or binge drinking. This means that the individual is usually getting drunk or high every weekend or more frequently. This is an addiction problem, and can have adverse effects on their body and mind. The physical long term effects can or may result in physical injuries, blackouts, memory loss, liver disease, stomach ulcers, high blood pressure, weight gain, impotence, brain damage and more. On the psychological side of things using drugs and/or alcohol frequently can and will start changing a person's personality.

Some of the changes can be immediate like memory loss, becoming irritable, having a short fuse, being aggressive or even becoming violent. Long term use will also change a person's outlook from positive to negative, cloud their judgement, decision making and suppress motivation. Other negative changes will affect an employee's presence, attitude, how they communicate with others, complain about work, change their team player attitude, drastically affect their productivity, quality of work and overall performance. It can adversely affect their work relationships, future opportunities, by breaking relations, or completely destroying them altogether.

This destructive cycle also influences on a personal level. The person may have been happy, stable and content about life before the alcohol and drug problems entered the picture. Personality changes that occur may result in instability, inconsistency, large mood swings, irritability, being aggressive, violent, destroying relationships, and increased family problems or induce domestic violence and more.

Another point is if the person is caught drinking and driving; they will be charged with a driving under influence or DUI. The outcome of a DUI charge will vary according to geographic location. Regardless, a DUI will completely change their life. This offense usually results in a suspension or losing their driver's license, jail time, fines and a criminal record. Even worse, if the person charged drives for a living, or uses a company car, this will immediately impact their current employment and livelihood.

Another safety issue about recreational use of drugs and alcohol is it can or may eventually lead to doing drugs or alcohol at work. Being impaired or buzzed at work will compromise our safety, and of your colleagues. The reason is while operating any kind of machinery or being in a position to make critical worksite decisions in error may result in a serious injury or fatality. This reminds me of a couple of examples of workplace alcohol related problems.

One shocking example of using alcohol at the workplace was about two pilots about to fly from Scotland to Newark in August of 2016. However, they were reported and drug tested to find out they were both too drunk to fly. They were going to fly the plane and endanger all the passenger's lives regardless of how impaired they were. How comforting is that? Luckily they were reported and caught. If you would like more information about this story, the article can be found at the following URL:

http://nypost.com/2016/08/28/two-tipsy-pilots-arrested-for-being-too-drunk-to-fly/

I recall being part of a crew in Columbia to perform an inline survey on a pipeline. There were only five of us a project manager, electronics tech, data analyst and two mechanical techs. We were there to perform a service for an oil and gas company and the project was about two months in length. In the first week, set up our data processing "war room" and checked out a few sites until our equipment arrived. We arrived at the location at 7:00 am ready to start unpacking our equipment and start testing.

However, before we could enter the work location, the security guard held up a small purple velour bag and asked each one of us to pick a small numbered ball from the bag. I laughed and was the first; I picked a dark blue ball with the number one on it. Then Carlos our data analyst picked a ball that was bright red with no numbers. The guard immediately asked Carlos to proceed inside the security office to have an alcohol breathalyzer test. We were all outside waiting for him thinking nothing of it.

After a few minutes, Carlos came out of the office and said he failed the test. We all were surprised and said, "What, how did you fail?" The guard came outside to inform us that Carlos had three times an impaired level of alcohol. Carlos was instructed to leave the area and go back to the hotel until there was a decision made. An hour later he was expelled from the country immediately to return to our head office to face the consequences. To make a long story short, a short while after returning to the head office Carlos was fired for his alcohol problem with no option for rehabilitation or anything. Very unfortunate since he was a nice person.

So, even if there isn't any fatality or accidents, the employee may be lucky for now. However, when an accident or incident does happen an immediate investigation will be carried out to determine the cause. A general investigation will include the safety officer inspecting, procedures, the accident area and interviewing all immediate personnel involved as well as, witnesses. Then drug testing is performed because it assists investigators in determining whether drugs or alcohol were part of the cause.

Testing, Testing... 1 – 2 – 3

It doesn't matter how much you study for this test if you fail it is indicative of a current or potential addiction problem. Testing is usually a urine test which is the cheapest method to use for employers. Drug testing is, used for the immediate detection of drugs and when public road accident fatalities occur, erratic driving behavior, as well as, workplace accidents or fatalities. This means testing is in regard to urgency.

Testing may also be initiated when an employee's behaviors become noticeably erratic and extreme. This would include, missing work all the time or being late, their demeanor is negative, rageful, or they become very argumentative and/or even violent. These kinds of behavior usually initiate an interview with their supervisor. The supervisor will inquire about what kind of problem they have at home or at work and may request a drug test to check if it is a contributing factor.

Alternately, drug screening is used for the assessment or analysis of drug use, preventive measures and as a deterrent. Employers generally conduct pre-employment screening of future employees in order to prevent hiring individuals who have drug or alcohol problems.

Random drug screening used by employers is very effective to deter or discourage current employees from using alcohol or drugs, and to maintain a drug and alcohol free workplace environment. Drug screening reduces health care costs, and worksite injuries or fatalities. It also plays a vital role in early detection of employee drug or alcohol problems. This allows employers to help them deal with their addiction by offering counselling services. Moreover, screening also upholds their consistency, work quality and productivity.

When employers use regular drug screening this ensures the company provides a safe workplace for employees and the public. Employers also maintain good standing and compliance with state, federal or provincial laws and also meet client requirements or standards. Having a drug free workplace reduces the employer's costs for worker's compensation, lowers liability insurance rates, and worker injury claims. Overall drug screening has its benefits but it's never foolproof.

Some Testing Facts

The drug testing techniques used by labs have certain detection thresholds and each drug they test has a certain timeframe for "positive" results. For instance, alcohol is detectable; however the amount that stays in the blood stream is a very short period of time which is usually about twenty-four hours. Therefore twenty-four hours later you would pass an alcohol test.

Drug tests also cover narcotics, such as, cocaine, Amphetamines, Heroin, Opiates and PCP. Cocaine stays in a user's system for about twenty-four hours like alcohol and is then not traceable. However, frequent or chronic users of cocaine have detectible levels in their system from 48 to 72 hours. This may be a short period of time just like alcohol levels but chances are the problem will still come to roost at some point especially with random drug testing.

The same tests also cover popular cannabinoid based drugs that have THC like, marijuana, hash, weed-oil or hash oil that stay in a user's system for prolonged periods far longer than cocaine or alcohol. THC can be traced up to a few weeks after usage and chronic users will fail testing up to 12 weeks later. The time frame for detection is equivalent to how much you have consumed. The reason is marijuana stays within the fat cells of your body unlike other drugs. Keep in mind that with any drug test, the lab provides your employer with full documentation about test results.

For instance, let's say you are a user and passed the drug test. This means that the level of drugs or alcohol in your system was lower than the test threshold level. For example the threshold level for a marijuana drug test or THC is usually 50 Nano-grams per milliliter or ng/ml. So if you passed that could mean that you still have a level of 35 ng/ml. This is included in the report that is given to your employer and clearly lets your employer know that you are a user. If you would like to read an excellent report called, The CBHSQ Report that is based on workplace statistics by the Substance Abuse and Mental Health Services Administration go to the following URL:

http://www.samhsa.gov/data/sites/default/files/report_1959/ShortReport-1959.html

Even with the new laws legalizing cannabis in many states and countries, companies will conform to using a zero tolerance policy instead of guessing at what levels are allowable, or who is under the influence and who is not. The only solution to drug testing I see is abstinence of any drugs or alcohol because if you lose your job over drug or alcohol problems you will have a very difficult time finding another job. Sure eventually you will find a job but it will be at some sweatshop that should have a revolving front door to support the high rate of employee turnover. Or you find a menial job that has nothing to do with your training or education and even better, you find a job with a company that doesn't drug test. Any way you look at it means that you value drugs and alcohol more than your career and livelihood.

It's all up to you of course to decide whether drugs and alcohol are a part of your life which can result in living a restricted lifestyle or abstain from drugs and alcohol and to be able to work for any company with a stable, promising future and exciting career! One word of advice is abstinence is your best friend when it comes to drugs and alcohol.

PHYSIO AND MASSAGE

This mainly applies to those employees who are continually sitting at a computer workstation day in day out or for those who perform repetitive physical work and tasks. I am referring to those that should have physio therapy and massage therapy on a regular basis. The best companies to get these services are from those that specialize with sports injuries. I have found that physio and massage therapists are the best people to have on your team because they will help you maintain your physical health. In fact, they have helped me all of my life to recover from injuries caused by car accidents, tornadoes, sports and work related pain and stiffness, as well as, other workplace injuries.

I personally have worked at a computer for almost two decades and I experience neck and back pain because of muscle stiffness. So once a week I visit a massage therapist to get loosened up. The worst thing I experienced was sciatica that was work related. This condition is caused by a herniated disc, bone spurs or when a nerve is compressed or if we sit all the time and don't do any exercise. With no exercise, we start losing our core muscle groups that include muscles in the abdomen, middle and lower back as well as, hips, shoulders and neck. These core muscles prevent sciatic nerve problems and are a part of keeping our posture correct.

When I started to have sciatica I had branching pain that extended through my lower back, hips, left butt cheek and down my left leg. My left leg had a painful dull numbness that was absolutely awful. I was taking painkillers for weeks which are horrible for your body and digestion. I went to a physio therapist to help me with the condition and after <u>one session</u> they reduced my pain level by at least 80 percent.

The physio therapist gave me some daily exercise's to do in order to build my core muscle strength which helped me combat sciatica. This condition was very painful and the pain was almost comparable to when I herniated one of my discs as I describe earlier in the Health and Safety section.

So having routine sessions with a massage therapist will be a big benefit for maintaining your good physical health. The cost is partially paid for by your employee benefits package and the rest of the cost can be put through your personal taxes as a deduction. Having a physical injury is not in anyone's best interest and using physio and massage as preventive maintenance for our body is a must for anyone.

OUTSIDE THE WORKPLACE

Each day we go into our workplace to perform our work duties. Many of us believe that once you have done your 8 hours you leave and that's it. We are done and off to our own world and to live our personal life. Sure, this is true but many employers are also concerned with the employee's behavior after work hours. The reason is employees are still representing the company. Even more so, if the employee is wearing a jacket with a small company logo or driving a company vehicle they can be identified and so can their employer.

Even though you're outside the workplace and living your personal life, you are always representing yourself in multiple identities as a:

- Person
- Employee
- Professional
- Neighbor
- Friend
- Acquaintance
- Spouse
- Mother or father

- Sister or brother

- Grandmother or grandfather

- Aunt or uncle or cousin

- Graduate from a high school, college, or university

- Resident of a village, town, city, state, province, region or country

So even though at times we may be wearing many of these hats, keep in mind that we are always representing the company we work for regardless of what time it is, or where we are, even if its domestically or internationally.

So with this in mind, be aware that companies have no tolerance of employees that are in the media like the news, radio, or internet, you tube, twitter, or Facebook, etc. when it is in regard to negative publicity. This kind of publicity will impact the company directly affecting its reputation because of its employee. Some impacts could be items such as, the company having dodgy employees, is untrustworthy, or is involved in fraudulent or other illegal exercises, like insider trading, embezzlement, money laundering, violence, or other criminal acts. Initially the company is smeared but can correct the false accusations through time however it still could significantly impact the company's stock price, vendors, and clients.

Some unacceptable situations for the company employee may include but are not limited to the following:

- Working a second job for a company that affects their work performance and productivity at their main employer

- Working for another company that is a direct competitor with your current company which poses as a conflict of interest

- Using company time and assets for their own part time business

- Incarcerated by police then missing work due to court appearances or imprisonment

- DUI charges when a vehicle is required for their job or they use a company vehicle

- Employee behavior, actions or conduct conflicts with the employer's mission and/or values

- Employees negative conduct is in public view and publicized either in, newspapers, TV news, or published in other venues

- When any employee behaviors and actions jeopardize the company's reputation

- The employee having a personal website or blog that is inappropriate, that is against company policies, values or morality

- Employees site or blog, has personal or professional content that is offensive in nature to the company, its clients or reflects badly on the company itself

- Employees secretly dating a colleague when it is in contradiction of company policy

- Workers engaging in criminal activity outside the workplace

- Employees with violent or sexual felonies

- Worker engaging in immoral or unethical conduct

- An employee posting, texting or emailing insulting and threatening comments aimed at his employer or other employees

- Soliciting colleagues at work about their own part-time business products and so on

- Workers using their employers name or influence for their own personal or part-time business benefit

- Selling or providing company proprietary or trade secret information to other companies, competitors or even to foreign governments

- Any fraudulent activities, like insider trading, money laundering, falsifying financial or legal documents etc.

Private, government or publicly traded companies require controlled and regulated media publicity. In fact, many companies have specific employees and departments in place to deal with any news releases or announcements. Companies that are publicly traded require press releases that are positive in nature and are fully invested to adhere to shareholder and stakeholder expectations. Any negative media attention can impact company stock prices and the company itself. This reminds me of a story regarding one of my employers.

Don't Have a Clue

I was working for a huge publicly traded company that in my opinion had a catastrophic security incident which compromised over sixty thousand employee's personal information. This is how it unfolded.

An individual employee was carrying around information with a carefree attitude with no idea of what they were holding. The employee copied personal employee data files for every worldwide employee onto their laptop as if it was any regular file, like a recipe, letter, picture, or joke, downloaded off the internet. They of course had placed the laptop in their car and were going to work on this information later at home possibly or maybe attend a meeting in a different city. Who knows? I sure don't.

Regardless, the employee files this person was carrying contained the following employee information:

- Name
- Address
- Date of Birth
- Employee number
- Bank Account number
- Direct Deposit details
- 401K account details
- Social Security Number
- Bank Branch details such as address, swift code, and/or routing number

Perpetrators broke into the employee's car and took the laptop that was loaded with vital employee payroll data. The HR manager sent a physical letter to each employee over a week after this theft occurred. The letter explained the situation about the laptop theft and details about what the laptop contained.

Upon receipt of the letter, I immediately contacted the company CEO via email and asked many questions verbatim, such as,

1. Why was this information on a laptop to begin with?
2. Why was it removed from the office?
3. How can this information be handled in such a careless way?
4. What procedures allow such inadequate handling of information like this?
5. Who is responsible for this and which department?
6. What are the costs associated with this mistake?
7. What changes can be made in procedures corresponding to vital information within the company?
8. Was this the lack of department personnel training?
9. Is this the irresponsibility of leadership in that department?
10. How long of a time period does this potential credit threat and identity theft to all employees last?
11. Why wasn't everyone notified immediately via email?
12. Why was there such a lax notification?
13. Was this information sold or stolen?

I also commented on the breach, asked that the employee, department VP and management team be fired for this irresponsible violation of employee payroll information that placed over 60,000 employees at risk of fraud and identity theft.

I also stated that I was aware of the sensitivity of this problem on how it relates to media leakage which would be devastating to the multi-billion dollar corporation, stakeholders, shareholders and its publicly traded stock price. The CEO contacted me via telephone and instructed me to not go to the police and file a theft or complaint since the media would immediately pick up on the situation and of course this would create havoc. I agreed.

The realities of this breach of employee payroll information gave thieves vital credit information to create and acquire false identities in order to conjure new credit cards, loans, lines of credit and other credit accounts to be used and/or sold to other people. This in effect would create 10s of millions of dollars in fraudulent loans, credit cards and lines of credit.

I found that many colleagues when asked about this breach had the general attitude of; "Nothing is going to happen its minor" as if they are immune to this type of potential crime. Many also thought it was minor and didn't care to create any waves or to protect themselves from identity theft activities.

I, on the other hand, immediately protected myself by registering with a credit agency and placed a fraud alert on my own credit file that is active for 6 years and set up notifications if any credit inquiries were made. I also closed my bank accounts, and cancelled credit cards and opened new ones. I didn't change my social security number because I wanted to wait to see if there was an indication of being compromised by these criminals.

The whole idea of this employee having a copy of this payroll information on a laptop was beyond belief. I say this because the information is so sensitive that only a couple of people within this multi-billion dollar corporation should actually have access to it, and it should be held on a computer that is off the grid, and not connected to any external internet or internal Ethernet connection. This computer with all this information should be locked behind closed doors that have a high-tech security system.

This whole experience proved that many employees within the company had no depth of what kind of information they were handling and had no protocols in place to protect it. I ended up quitting this company two weeks after because of this unrecoverable and irresponsible security breach of my information. This all happened outside the workplace after hours. I can only hope that this company immediately reviewed its policies in accordance with this huge embarrassment.

Companies have policies in place that employees must follow and conform to in order to remain employed. For that reason employees receive training about company policies, procedures, ethics, code of conduct, and other related company courses. These courses train their employees about bribery, ethics, etiquette, conflicts of interest, fraudulent activity and more.

So it's up to you to conform to company policies and be aware that your conduct in or out of the office does count. So if you are involved in some form of policy breach in regard to drug abuse, illegal activity, domestic violence or other situations your job may end abruptly. Keep in mind that being fired for this kind of situation is very hard to explain to a potential employer when looking for another job. So it's better to take it easy and have fun on your personal time, living life the way you want to because it does matter what you do outside of work hours.

CREDIT REPORTS

I am sure that many of you are questioning the title and asking, "Why are credit reports about best practices?" The answer is quite simple, credit reports are used by many employers as a part of their screening process.

According to the the Society of Human Resource Management (SHRM) almost half of employers use credit profiles as a part of their hiring process. Of those organizations just over half conduct credit checks after a job offer while a third obtain a credit check after an interview. Also over half of the organizations allowed job candidates explain the results of their credit checks before making a decision to hire or not.

This information strongly suggests that your credit report is important to almost half of the employers and may have you wondering if employers are looking at your full credit report information. First of all, according to the U.S. Fair Credit Reporting Act (FCRA), the company requires a written letter of consent by the candidate in order to pull an employment credit report. Most importantly the report information they receive from any of the three main credit bureaus *Equifax, Transunion*, and *Experian* is unlike a detailed standard credit report.

The actual report employers receive does not deduct points from the candidates credit score as other inquiries do. The report is referred to as an *employment credit report* which is not the same as the credit report you would see or what your bank would see.

In fact, the report is written to protect your privacy so it doesn't show your credit score, account numbers, date of birth and age. For example, a standard *Transunion* employment credit report shows the following details:

- Full Name

- Social Security Number

- Current and two previous addresses

- Phone Number

- Four Current and past employers, address, titles, dates of employment (upon availability)

- Notification of any civil judgements, tax liens or bankruptcies

- Unpaid bills turned over to collection agencies

- A record of candidates credit and payment patterns, includes date, company name, address and telephone number and

- Previous credit or employment inquiries that have made

However, the employer can also add many other optional information packages to the report as the following:

- Additional income information which adds IRA distributions, investment income, unemployment compensation and other sources

- Any instances regarding suspected fraud using social security numbers and/or suspicious addresses and

- An overview of candidates overall financial status

Many employment credit reports that are pulled by employers are usually for positions that require background checks and verification such as:

- Security based jobs or those with national security clearance requirements like, homeland security, national guard, military, security officers, police, security guards and other related security based jobs

- Financial based jobs or any jobs related to high trust responsibilities, or those involving money, such as, cashiers, tellers, banking staff, accountants, loans officers, stock and commodity market traders, and other related financial based jobs

- Senior executive positions such as CEO, CFO, CIO, VPs and employees that have access to highly confidential employee information

- Information based jobs that are responsible for highly sensitive information such as, medical records, benefits, salary, banking information, social security numbers, administrators, and IT

These employment credit checks are performed by companies to assist in making an accurate assessment of the potential new hire. The employment credit report shows an actual account of the candidate's overall level of integrity and trustworthiness and is used for early detection of their financial problems.

In other words, the report information is used to reduce the employer's risks when hiring new personnel. Some employers most common reasons for accessing a credit report are to:

- Decrease and prevent potential theft

- Lower and prevent the chances of embezzlement

- Reduce the company's legal liability for negligent hiring and

- Comply with local, state or federal laws

If you are wondering what "negligent hiring" is, it means that the company hired an individual with full knowledge and awareness about the employee's background being untrustworthy and dangerous. In this situation, the company itself would be responsible for that employee's actions. Therefore, when it comes to new hire, companies use credit reports to prevent, eliminate or to reduce their risk liability.

So what if your credit report has some negative aspects? Generally this would signify that you have deficiencies in upholding financial responsibilities. The question is does this affect the candidate's chances of getting hired? It might but according to the SHRM only a small percentage of employers didn't hire individuals who had negative details on their report. While the majority of companies focused on these main hiring fundamentals:

- Candidate has previous work experience related to the job their being hired to do

- Interviewers feel that candidate is a good fit for the job and organization

- Candidate has the required specific skill sets required for the job

So, overall a credit report may impact your chances of getting hired. Also be aware that you can always review your own credit report to verify that it is accurate with no error. If your credit report has discrepancies, report them immediately to the credit agency to update the information so you have an accurate credit report. This update can be done over the phone.

Keep in mind that it's in your best interest to have a good credit report and rating regardless if a company pulls a report or not. Since, having a good credit report helps you in many areas of your life such as, obtaining credit cards, lines of credit, and mortgages and can help you get that awesome job you want.

IT'S A FIT

Yes it's a fit. I found this to be a key best practice because it refers to an employee, "fitting in" with an employer and the organization. This best practice is to save yourself from entering into an employment situation that really isn't for you. However, I have found that during an interview process there are many indicators that help us to make a decision based on whether we fit in or not.

First of all trying to get a feel for what is actually going on in an interview is quite difficult because the candidate is simultaneously trying to read the interviewer and themselves. After taking in all of this information, the candidate has to discern whether they fit with the company and organization or not; which is all based on how they felt during the interview, what the interviewers were saying as well as, the overall atmosphere of the interview. In addition, the candidate must also take into account the way they felt before going into the interview.

I found that before jumping to conclusions taking into account how you felt before going into the interview, like in fear, anxiety, don't like the company or don't know why you agreed to attend the interview and so on. For instance, if you already know from past experience that this employer's pay is noncompetitive, or they don't offer a benefits package, or the hours are not suitable and so on. It also maybe that you feel you don't have the experience or skills to fulfill the job requirement, or doubt yourself. With this in mind you already have a bias and expectations that are somewhat negative even before going into an interview. So take note because these will determine whether you are a fit.

The second pointer is based on your own intuition or gut feeling since it's a part of your innate guidance system. Our intuition generally protects us by providing physical feedback without thinking. This can in fact be a tingle, a gut feeling, or feeling that a situation is not right, uncomfortable, or people are untrustworthy, or we don't feel safe and so on. These are important to us because if something doesn't feel right, it probably isn't right even though you may not be able to instantly pinpoint what isn't right.

Another aspect is to observe the interviewer's attitude, body language and the energy in the room. For instance, if the person conducting the interview seems to be happy, attentive, easy going, professional, polite, unscripted and soft spoken it is positive. This would suggest they are very comfortable with their jobs, appreciate having you in an interview, enjoy speaking to you and have a genuine interest. This kind of atmosphere and interaction of course is very positive.

On the other hand you may feel that the interviewers are stressed, impatient, nervous, or disorganized. This may implicate that the interviewers under pressure to meet deadlines, scripted, biased, do not enjoy what they do and would rather be doing something else or could be unhappy with the employer, etc. This is not a positive environment and should be taken into account.

Another point is when it's as if the interviewer is talking down to you making you feel worthless, that your education and experience is of little value that you and other's like yourself are a dime a dozen or the interviewer is boasting about other candidates that have superior experience. If that is the case it is very negative in nature and inexcusable. They may be using this tactic to make you feel worthless in order to have you possibly agree for a reduced salary or hourly rate. They could also be putting you down in order to feel better about themselves. Another angle could be that they just don't like you or are envious because of your youth, good looks, perfect hair, skill sets, experience, wonderful physique, your suit or dress, etc. Regardless, this is still negative and unacceptable behavior on their part which reminds me of an interview I had.

I recall having an interview with one of the largest companies in the world and the regional manager was conducting the interview. During the interview the manager asked me about Microsoft software applications and I simply answered, "Yes I am proficient with Word, Excel, Access, Project, Visio, PowerPoint, and Publisher..." then he rudely said, "Who cares my 9 year old son knows all of those too! Do you know anything else?" After I heard and felt these belittling comments, I immediately stood up and looked at the manager straight in the eyes and said, "Not interested" and abruptly ended the interview and walked out. I did this because of the offensive and unnecessary behavior of the manager, besides do I want to work for a moron like this? "Not in this lifetime!"

Another scenario could be that during the interview as they are explaining details about the role, duties and functions, that you get energized strongly suggests that the job suits your interests, passions and expectations, which of course are a bonus.

Another item to mention is while in the interview if you feel uncomfortable or uneasy or even pressured it would suggest that maybe the company and the individual conducting the interview are feeling the same about working for the organization and may even complain to you about their job. This could strongly suggest that the employees may be under pressure and overworked with no work-life balance regardless of the information relayed in the interview.

Also, in some circumstances you may feel like you are being interrogated instead of interviewed. Keep in mind that some people are very direct which may seem like they are interrogating you but in reality they are not. However, if they interrogated you, speak up and ask them if they usually conduct interviews or if they are filling in for someone. You can also ask if they had problems in prior interviews with candidates. They in turn may ask why you are asking the questions. The reason is you feel like you're being interrogated and not interviewed. Generally this kind of interview suggests that the interviewer may not believe you, your experience and qualifications. This strongly suggests this is not a suitable organization to work for in my opinion just based on the unprofessional conduct of the interviewer and is displaying frustration, anger and disbelief in your credentials. When there is no mutual trust, you and they have nothing in common.

Another aspect to take into account is to ask questions about the company, the job, tasks, pay, holidays, start date, who your supervisor is, or who will report to you, how many reports you have, if there is travel involved, if they can't answer questions that you ask, this would suggest they are not informed or are trying to make up answers instead of telling the truth about the real work environment, organization and morale.

Most importantly ask the interviewer why they are hiring for this particular position, by asking if someone quit and if so why, is it due to expansion, a new position, new division, department, etc. The answer to this question will reveal more detail about what's really going on, because when someone quits and there is no one to work with you to do knowledge transfer, it sends a clear message that things are not as they appear.

If the interviewer does not offer a tour of the facility, offices and work area to meet future colleagues then request a tour and if they refuse, this maybe a red flag and take note. However they may have a legitimate reason for this. Why request a tour? A tour reveals a lot of information about the organization, work environment, employees, and morale.

This is a big indicator of the companies' true work environment. The reason is while touring, the reaction of the employees will clearly show the real work environment. For instance, if the employees do not say anything to you or the interviewer, then this indicates there is unrest, dissatisfaction amongst employees and low morale. On the other hand, if many employees say hello, joke with the interviewer by making comments and roasting the interviewer and even you in a good hearted way then this is very positive.

Also during your interview or after, you can make up your own conclusions based on asking yourself and the interviewer a series of questions such as:

1. Is this a new position? If so, how much work is there to support long-term employment?
2. If this is an existing position what happened to the last employee who held this position and why did the employee leave?
3. What does your intuition or gut feeling tell you?
4. How did you feel while speaking to the person or people in the interview?
5. Was the information in the interview something that made you excited, eager, or happy to work for this organization?
6. Did the interviewer seem happy, easy going and was frequently smiling?
7. Did you feel the interviewer was a good listener or preoccupied as if they were somewhere else?
8. Did the interviewer seem agitated, frustrated, angry, and rude?
9. Were you comfortable and relaxed in the interview or feeling uneasy and somewhat pressured?
10. Did you feel like you were being interrogated instead of being interviewed?
11. What was the atmosphere like, negative or, positive?
12. Did you feel that you finally found a company that understands you and others like you as far as

communication, pay, employee treatment, benefits, etc.?
13. Are the company's values and ethics similar to your own?
14. Does it sound like a true team environment?
15. Do you seem to hit it off with the people conducting the interview?
16. Are the questions reasonable and fair?
17. Did they give you ample time to answer any questions about your prior work or even your employment credit report?
18. Are there any indications of urgency for hiring a candidate? If so, how long was this position being considered and why haven't they hired anyone until now?
19. Why are they hiring? Is it a new contract, client, new expansions like a division, department or a strategic move?
20. Why are they hiring? Is it just to have people in place just in case they get the new contract?
21. How many new positions are there?
22. How often does the company hire people?
23. Is there a large turnaround of employees?
24. Are you hiring more than one person? If so why are there so many and is there enough work long-term to support all people being hired?
25. Are you hiring two people for the same position only to let one of the employees go later on?
26. Did the interviewer make you feel that your experience and qualification were not that valuable

or make you feel worthless? If so, directly confront the interviewer and ask why they are discounting your experience and making you feel that your experience means very little or is unworthy.

Even if we attempt to analyze the information in the interview it's not full proof because certain people lie by omission very well and can fool many. Of course, some of us have an innate ability to read between the lines which is very important and helps us tremendously. Some of the common qualities of a candidate that are most important to employers are related to work experience, specific skill sets, certifications, education, interview performance and having excellent work references.

However, even though there are many factors involved, all of these are worthless if there is no "fit". In other words, regardless of how much education, experience, certifications, and how good your references are and background is; if you don't have a fit you have nothing. Unfortunately it's time to move on to the next opportunity. For example, I recall having an interview for a company and during the interview process the questions they asked were technical in nature but revealed they were actually seeking a candidate with a different skill set. In other words, the interviewers didn't really know who they were looking for otherwise I wouldn't have been selected for an interview.

As a rule of thumb, all attitudes, actions and atmosphere at each workplace or organization is a reflection of the management style of higher-ups. So, the way they manage the organization trickles down to everyone and is revealed by the employee's attitudes, work performance, employee turnover rate and morale.

ME, MYSELF AND I

This best practice is all about you and what you like to do. What makes you happy that puts a smile across your face from ear to ear? When do you get lost in what you're doing by losing track of time and even your surroundings? Does it involve being creative like, painting, drawing, programming, or writing? Could it be examining financials, spreadsheets, helping people medically, or riding on a fire engine going to a fire or maybe putting on your police uniform excited to know what adventures your new day brings while putting your life on the line?

What this means is that you are doing something that is based one or a combination of your passions, something that you love to do that makes you feel excited with time passing quickly without having any self-awareness. It all comes easy to you, effortless as if you were given a gift to perform that particular passion. While others educated and specialists in that particular area have difficultly. This free-flowing mindset is what the author Mihaly Csikszentmihalyi (pronounced "Me-high-Cheek-sent-me-high") described in his book entitled, "Flow".

The state of flow is a highly focused mental state of concentration. This is having clarity of a challenge, while all of your energy and focus is on the actions you are performing. Your time is lost, and what you are doing is rewarding. This is a basic description of being in the state of flow.

With that in mind, this best practice is to find work or to choose a profession that is one of your passions. The reason is, you will be excited to go to work every day, it doesn't feel like work, has no stress and you will feel fulfilled and happy every day. As you continue to work, time will fly while you are having the best time of your life but oddly enough it won't feel right to you because you are actually getting paid to have fun. It doesn't get any better than this.

Personally, I would rather hire a person who is passionate about a certain profession that may even be self-taught rather than someone with a diploma or degree in the same profession. The reason is, "flow" and it is a gift imbedded within the person so the commitment, drive and quality of work is by far the best of the best.

Richard Renstone

IT'S A WRAP

This wraps up *Make Your Career Great Again!* In *Part I*, we examined what it means to be an employee and the general mindset permanent employees have. We continued by discussing the advantages and disadvantages of being an employee and also exposed some of the secrets employees have believed for years; which have been a controlling force in employee's lives both on the job front and financially. In *Part II*, we explored over 50 game changing employee best practices that are the best or most effective way or method of performing certain tasks or procedures at the workplace.

Working is a large part of life and at times, a lot of it may be frustrating and unfair but on the other hand it can be very rewarding, uplifting, fun and fulfilling especially when you have a positive outlook and follow your heart.

This book has given you knowledge, understanding and a series of ideas that can *make your career great again* and in turn *make your life great again*! The only way to change your current situation and future is by taking action today. Keep in mind changes don't happen overnight and require your full attention and most importantly a commitment. I can only stress that truth; honesty and integrity are the ultimate qualities of all.

Before saying good-bye I would leave you with a note:

If you are fed up and considering a change from being an employee and have been thinking about becoming a contractor then, look for my new book series on contracting because you will be absolutely shocked at what you have been missing all these years! See you there!

Thanks for letting me enter your life and God Bless!

Many thanks,

Richard Renstone

ABOUT THE AUTHOR

Richard Renstone grew up in a small northern city in Canada, and completed an associate's degree in Electronics Engineering.

Soon after, Renstone acquired a job in the oil and gas industry, launching him into various countries in South America, Europe, Middle East, Far East and Australia during which evaded death upon two occasions.

A decade later, Renstone changed careers to become a technical publication author and instructional designer. During this time he acquired two undergraduate degrees, a Bachelor of Arts and Bachelor of Metaphysical Science. Renstone is a lifelong learner and continues to acquire specialized knowledge and certifications.

Today Renstone is a writer, author, and has published many books and will continue to write and travel the world.

If you have any comments or questions please feel free to contact me via email at richardrenstone@gmail.com or find me on Twitter @RichardRenstone

Richard Renstone

Page Left Blank

OTHER BOOKS BY THE AUTHOR

Permanent Employee: The Pros, Cons and Secrets (2018)

Permanent Employee: Best Practices Handbook (2018)

Make Your Career Great Again! (2018)

www.ingramcontent.com/pod-product-compliance
Lightning Source LLC
Chambersburg PA
CBHW032038090426
42744CB00004B/57